S

Transitioning a

Page 2

Section 2
Goal Setting and Learning
Page 118

Section 3
Learning and Assessment Preparation
Page 248

Section 4
Study Journal
Page 318

A LEARNING AND STUDENT
SUPPORT PROGRAMME

Name: _____

Class: _____

School: _____

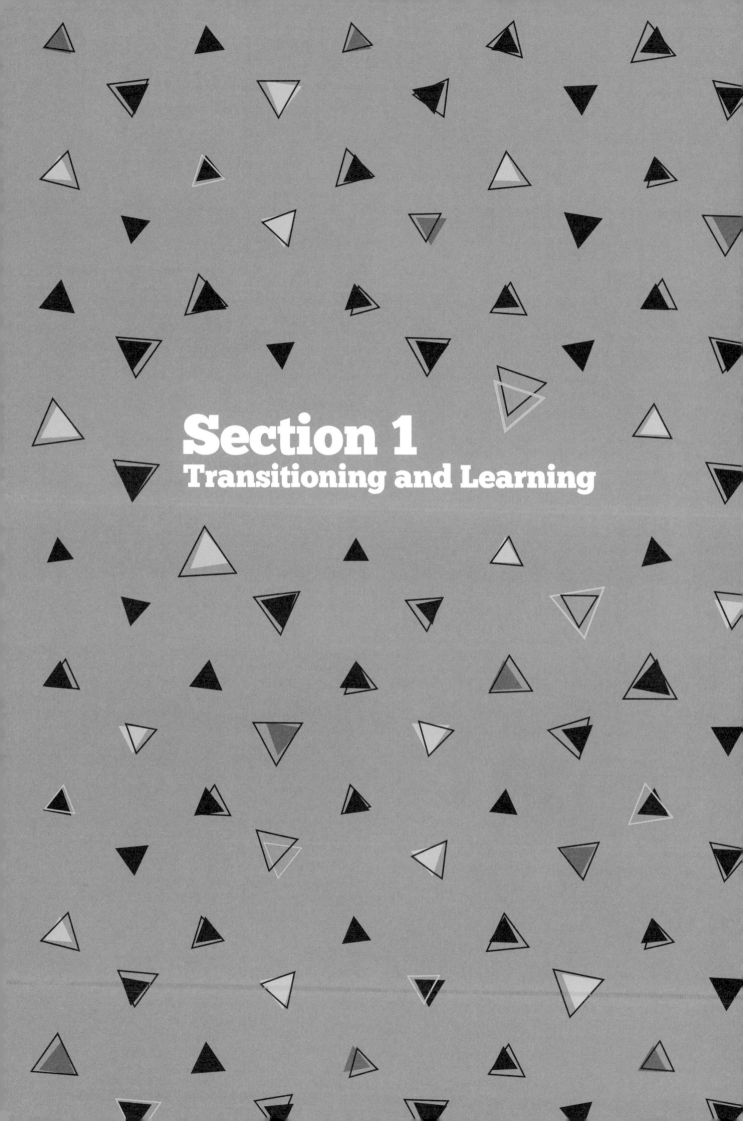

Section 1
Transitioning and Learning

Introduction

The sooner you can settle into your new regime in school, the sooner you begin to make progress in your learning and study.

The focus for this section is to assist you the student in settling into your school and to provide you with practical techniques that will help you learn better. This section is broken up into three key areas:

1. **Transitioning and settling in**
   Chapters 1 and 2 will help you settle more quickly into your new school and routine. It explores your new subjects and how to become more organised in your learning at school and at home.

2. **What learning is all about**
   The next two chapters help you understand better how you actually learn. You will explore how your brain works along with the skills and behaviours you can develop which assist you in becoming a better learner.

3. **Managing information**
   In secondary school you are presented with lots of new information in your various subjects. The key to being successful in your learning is to practise simple techniques that will help you manage all this information. This last section is divided into four chapters, which are:

   I. *Managing Information: Listening*
   You take in a lot of information by listening to the teacher and others in your class. Listening is a skill which you can develop and practise. This chapter will help you do just that so that you are paying attention to what you need to learn.

   II. *Managing Information: Reading.*
   Now that you have begun to understand how information is organised you can begin to engage more with the various pieces of text you come across in your text books and other places. You learn how to read with purpose to identify the information you need from a piece of text.

   III. *Managing Information: Thinking*
   In this chapter you begin to think about and understand how the information is arranged, how each subject is broken down into topics and even further into keywords that you need to remember.

   IV. *Managing Information: Note taking and answering*
   Here you look at how to break down the information you have read by creating your own notes. You also look at some simple tools called writing frames that will help you be more efficient in answering questions on a piece of text you have read.

Finally, there is an end of section reflection for you to reflect on what it is you have personally learned from this section, not just in the workbook but also in your engagement with other students when you were undertaking some of the various exercises. This reflection will help improve your learning and study going forward.

You are given the opportunity to practise all these new skills with some of the subjects you are studying for the Junior Cycle.

Section 1
Transitioning and Learning

Chapter 1
Settling In

Chapter 2
Subjects and Homework

Chapter 3
My Brain and Learning

Chapter 4
Behaviours for Learning

Chapter 5
Managing Information: Listening

Chapter 6
Managing Information: Reading

Chapter 7
Managing Information: Thinking

Chapter 8
Managing Information: Note taking and writing

End of Section Reflection

Chapter 1
Settling In

Lesson 1
MY TIMETABLE

Aim To learn how to effectively use your school timetable

 Learning Point 1 My own timetable

The school day can appear quite busy and confusing initially, trying to figure out where you are supposed to be and when. With new subjects, in different classrooms and with different teachers, it can be quite confusing. Most schools hand out timetables to students with abbreviations of the subject and teachers' initials simply to fit everything in; you may need help in decoding all these new abbreviations.

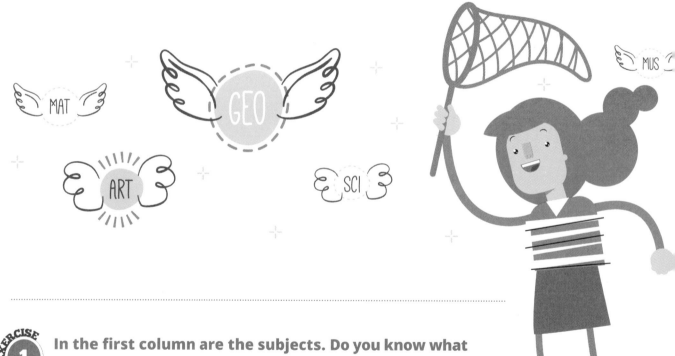

EXERCISE 1 In the first column are the subjects. Do you know what the abbreviations are for all your subjects?

Try to fill in the following grid with the abbreviations of each subject, the room number/name and the teacher's name/initials. There are spaces at the end to add additional subjects.

Subject	Abbreviations	Room	Teacher	Teacher Initials
Gaeilge (Irish)				
English				
Maths				
French				
History				
Business Studies				
Geography				
Technical Graphics				
Social Personal and Health Education				
Religion				
Civic, Social and Political Education				
Science				
Metalwork				
Spanish				
Home Economics				
Technology				
Physical Education				

Understanding your Timetable

This is a sample timetable with the subjects, locations and times of each class. Study this timetable and see if you can answer the questions that follow.

SCHOOL TIMETABLE

TIME	MON		TUE		WED		THU		FRI	
9.00–9.40	ENG	R1	GAE	R14	HI	R3	METAL	MR	PE	GYM
9.40–10.20	SCI	LAB3	RE	R11	SCI	LAB3	METAL	MR	ART	ART R.
10.20–10.55	HIS	R6	MAT	R3	MAT	R3	GEO	R10	MAT	R3
10.55–11.10	BREAK									
11.10–11.50	GAE	R14	EN	R1	BUS	R5	GAE	R14	RE	R11
11.50–12.25	MUS	MUSIC R	FREN	R7	ENG	R1	ENG	R1	HIS	R3
12.25–13.05	SPHE	R20	PE	GYM	CSPE	R2	MAT	R3	FREN	R7
13.05–13.45	LUNCH									
13.45–14.25	MAT	R3	BUS	R5	FREN	R7	ART	ART R.	ENG	R1
14.25–15.05	FREN	R7	ART	ART R.	GAE	R14	BUS	R5	GEO	R10
15.05–15.45	GEO	R10	HIS	R3	RE	R11	SCI	LAB3	GAE	R14

a. How often does this student have Religion in the week?

b. In what room is the Science class held?

c. How many periods of English does this student have?

d. What class has this student got at 12.25 on Friday?

e. Where is this student supposed to be on Wednesday at 14.25?

Learning Point 2   My own timetable

How familiar are you already with your own timetable?

EXERCISE 3

Cover your timetable and do not look at it for the answers. Try and answer as many of the following questions as possible, how many did you get right?

a. School begins at what time?

b. How many periods do you have each day?

c. How long is each period?

d. How many times a week do you have English?

e. How many periods are there between the break time and lunchtime?

f. Lunchtime begins at what time and finishes at what time?

g. How many periods of SPHE do you have each week?

h. What classroom do you have Geography in?

i. How many periods a week do you have for Geography?

j. School finishes at what time?

k. What class do you have after lunch on a Wednesday?

l. What subject do you have last period of the week?

EXERCISE 4

As a quick recap and summary of the lesson, fill in the following summary table of your timetable and subjects.

Subject	What is the Subject?	Number of Classes	Who is my Teacher?
Ir / Gae			
Eng			
Maths			
Sci			
Bus			
Hist			
Geog			
MTW			
MTM			
RE			
CSPE			
SPHE			
TG			
Music			
Art			

(i) Do you have a favourite subject yet? ☐ Yes ☐ No

(ii) Why?

_____

_____

_____

_____

(iii) What new subject are you looking forward to finding out more about?

_____

(iv) Why?

_____

_____

_____

PAUSE AND REFLECT

1. What have you learned in this lesson?

_____

_____

2. How did you learn this?

_____

_____

3. How can you use what you learned in your schoolwork/study?

_____

_____

MENTAL NOTE

"Develop a passion for learning. If you do you will never cease to grow." – Anthony J. D'Angelo

Chapter 1
Settling In

Lesson 2
BEING ORGANISED

Aim To help you organise yourself both in school and at home

Learning Point 1

Sometimes you have so many things to do that you can either forget something or end up somewhere at the wrong time. As a result you might end up missing part of a class or end up having the wrong books and materials with you.

EXERCISE 1 **a. School day** – This exercise helps you understand how you spend your time during a typical school day. Please fill in the blanks in the diagram.

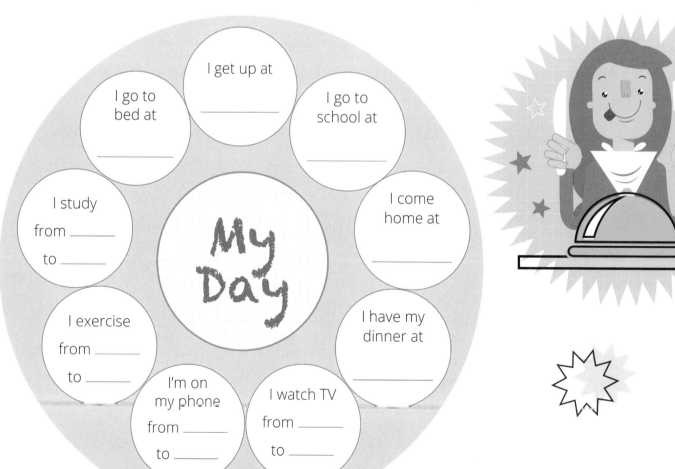

I get up at _____

I go to bed at _____

I go to school at _____

I study from _____ to _____

My Day

I come home at _____

I exercise from _____ to _____

I have my dinner at _____

I'm on my phone from _____ to _____

I watch TV from _____ to _____

b. Weekend – As everybody's weekend tends to be slightly different there are more blanks here. Please fill in the blanks in the diagram.

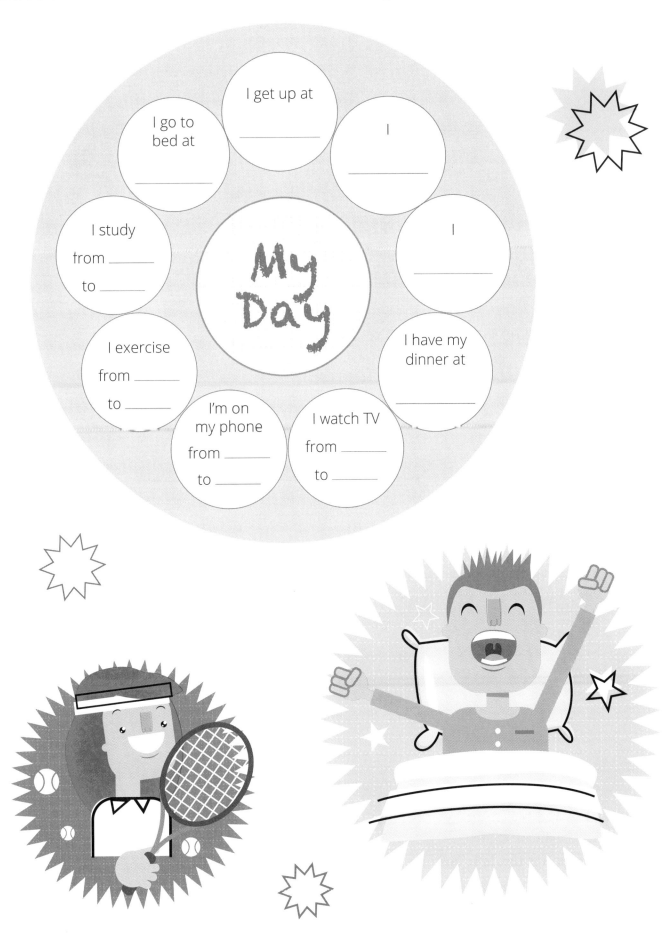

I go to
bed at
_____

I get up at
_____

I
_____

My
Day

I study
from _____
to _____

I
_____

I exercise
from _____
to _____

I have my
dinner at
_____

I'm on
my phone
from _____
to _____

I watch TV
from _____
to _____

EXERCISE 2 Now fill in the 24-hour clock, highlight anything that is compulsory in **red** and anything that is optional in **yellow**.

24-hour	Weekdays	Weekends
00.00 - 06.00		
07.00		
08.00		
09.00		
10.00		
11.00		
12.00		
13.00		
14.00		
15.00		
16.00		
17.00		
18.00		
19.00		
20.00		
21.00		
22.00		
23.00		
24.00		

a. When completed did you notice anything?

_____

b. Are you surprised by the amount of free time you have?

☐ **Yes** ☐ **No**

c. What does this tell you?

_____

_____

EXERCISE 3 Now develop a timetable for your normal week, ensuring that you have enough time for both study and recreation.

NORMAL WEEK TIMETABLE

TIME	MON	TIME	TUE	TIME	WED	TIME	THU	TIME	FRI

EXERCISE 4

Being on Time Questionnaire

Time management and punctuality are really important skills you need to develop. Here is a checklist to help you reflect on how good you are at being on time.

Are you the type of person that is good at being on time? Let us see! Answer the following questions as honestly as possible.

a. Are you usually on time for things, like meeting friends, going to training, catching the bus for school? ☑ **Yes** ☐ **No**

b. Out of 10, how would you rate yourself for being on time?

    1   2   3   4   5   6   7   8   9 **(10)**

c. Can you remember a time that you had to wait for someone or something that was late? ☐ **Yes** ☐ **No**

How did you feel and what happened?

_____

d. Do you find it hard to get up in the morning? ☐ **Yes** ☐ **No**

e. How do you wake up in the mornings?

_____

_____

f. Out of 10, how would you rate yourself for being on time for school?

    1   2   3   4   5   6   7   8   9   10

g. What happens when other students are late for school?

_____

_____

h. Out of 10, how would you rate yourself for being on time for class?

    1   2   3   4   5   6   7   8   9   10

i. What do you do if you are late when you have to go into one of your classes?

_____

_____

j. What excuses are given when people are late for classes?
    Write down as many as you can think of.

_____

_____

_____

k. How many of these excuses have you used and how often?

_____

_____

_____

l. What would help you to improve your time keeping for school or class?

_____

_____

_____

m. Having answered these questions do you think you are a good time keeper or time manager?   ☐ Yes ☐ No
    Give reasons for your answer.

_____

_____

n. If you are not good at managing time, write down three things you think you can do in the future to improve.

    (i) _____

    (ii) _____

    (iii) _____

Learning Point 2 | Equipment

Being organised is a key skill that leads to effective study behaviour. The sooner you take responsibility for organising yourself the better the outcomes for your time spent learning both in school and at home.

EXERCISE 5

My school locker, My school bag, My desk at home

This exercise will help you to think about what various items you need each day and where you should store them.

In the diagram write in the items you think you should have in each place.

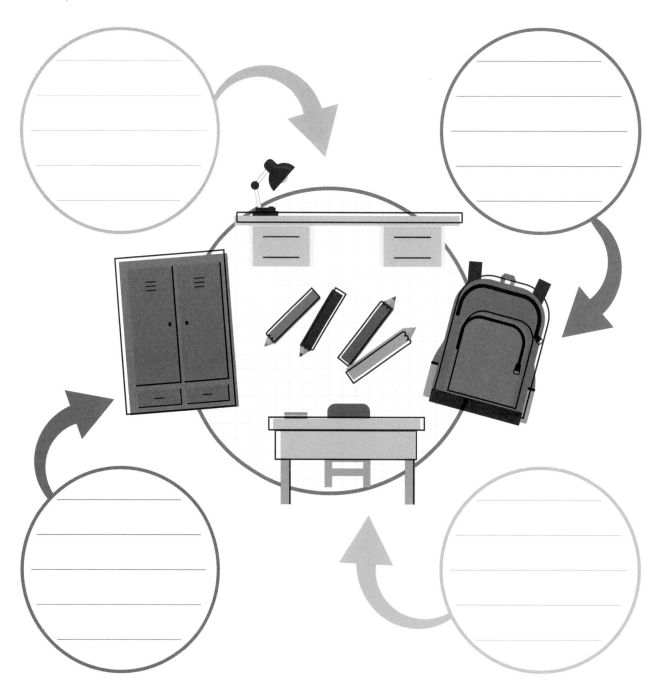

Checklists

Checklists can help you become more organised. You can have a checklist of things to do in the morning, evening, etc. so that you will remember what you need to do. Some people bring a shopping list with them when they go shopping so they remember what to buy. Once you start doing this every day it will become a habit and you will not need the checklist after a short time.

Use the **templates** to design your own checklists, which you can cut out and stick somewhere you can see them.

MORNING CHECKLIST

- ☑ Full uniform, tie, school jacket, shoes?
- ☑ Do I have my locker key and swipe card?
- ☑ Do I have all my books/zip files for class?
- ☑ Do I need my PE gear, ingredients, Art pack?
- ☑ Is my schoolbag packed and ready, lunch?

EVENING CHECKLIST

- ☑ Full uniform, tie, school jacket, shoes?
- ☑ Do I have my locker key and swipe card?
- ☑ Have I done all my homework for tomorrow's class?
- ☑ Do I need my PE gear, ingredients, Art pack?
- ☐

MORNING CHECKLIST

- ☐ Full uniform, tie, school jacket, shoes?
- ☐ Do I have my locker key and swipe card?
- ☐ Do I have all my books/zip files for class?
- ☐ Do I need my PE gear, ingredients, Art pack?
- ☐ Is my schoolbag packed and ready, lunch?
- ☐ _____
- ☐ _____

EVENING CHECKLIST

- ☐ Full uniform, tie, school jacket, shoes?
- ☐ Do I have my locker key and swipe card?
- ☐ Have I done all my homework for tomorrow's class?
- ☐ Do I need my PE gear, ingredients, Art pack?
- ☐ _____
- ☐ _____
- ☐ _____

PAUSE AND REFLECT

1. What have you learned in this lesson?

   _____

   _____

2. How did you learn this?

   _____

   _____

3. How can you use what you learned in your schoolwork/study?

   _____

   _____

Chapter 1
Settling In

Lesson 3

FILLING IN MY HOMEWORK JOURNAL

Aim — To help you make effective use of your homework journal as a resource for organising your school life and study

 Learning Point 1

The homework journal tends to be the main means of communication between your school and home but also has many other important jobs like helping you organise yourself and providing important information about the school.

It is good to take time to explore your homework journal, understand what it contains, and be able to use it effectively.

 EXERCISE 1

My Homework Journal Contents

Look at the contents of your school journal. Do you know what each section is about? Try and fill in the following information using the template below.

→ The name of each section

→ A short description of what it contains

→ A short description of how this can help you

My Homework Journal – Table of Contents

a. **Section 1:** _____

   Contains: _____

   Useful because... _____

b. **Section 2:** _____

   Contains: _____

   Useful because... _____

c. **Section 3:** _____

   Contains: _____

   Useful because... _____

d. **Section 4:** _____

   Contains: _____

   Useful because... _____

e. **Section 5:** _____

   Contains: _____

   Useful because... _____

f. **Section 6:** _____

   Contains: _____

   Useful because... _____

g. **Section 7:** _____

   Contains: _____

   Useful because... _____

h. **Section 8:** _____

   Contains: _____

   Useful because... _____

i. **Section 9:** _____

   Contains: _____

   Useful because... _____

Learning Point 2 *Good Homework Journal Usage*

Sometimes at the end of class you can scribble down some rough notes about your homework and end up that night scratching your head trying to make out what you recorded. It is good to write down as much detail as possible in your journal in clear handwriting to make sure you don't forget anything. Below is a checklist of the key elements of effective use of your homework journal.

Good journal entries

A good journal has the following:

→ Details of material covered in class
→ Details of homework given, if any
→ Details of when homework is due to be handed up
→ Clear handwriting
→ Parent's signature if expected.

Subject	Homework/learning outcomes
English	Comprehension on Leonardo Di Caprio Q. 1 - 6 Due Tues
Maths	Fractions Q. 11, 12, 14 p. 49 Due Tues
French	Ma Famile, Learn vocabulary at end of chapter p. 27
Tech Graph.	Elevation plan drawing Q. 3 p. 18 Due Fri
History	The work of an archaeologist - No homework
To remember	PE kit for tomorrow
Teacher's comment:	
Parent's signature:	

EXERCISE 2

Now over to you:

a. Using what you have just learned, create a good journal entry based on your last entry.

Subject	Homework/learning outcomes
Teacher's comment:	
Parent's signature:	

b. Does your journal entry look different from what you have been filling in up until now?

☐ **Yes** ☐ **No**

Explain the difference: _____

_____

PAUSE AND REFLECT

1. What have you learned in this lesson?

_____

_____

2. How did you learn this?

_____

_____

3. How can you use what you learned in your schoolwork/study?

_____

_____

MENTAL NOTE

"Education is the most powerful weapon which
you can use to change the world." – Nelson Mandela

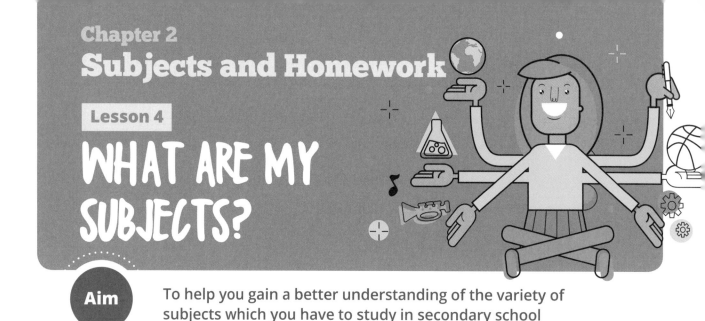

Chapter 2
Subjects and Homework

Lesson 4
WHAT ARE MY SUBJECTS?

Aim — To help you gain a better understanding of the variety of subjects which you have to study in secondary school

Learning Point 1

Another big adjustment for you is the number of new subjects you have to engage with. Many of these are unfamiliar. Everyone has their favourite subjects, subjects that they enjoy more than others. You might find that the more you get into a subject the more you grow to like it. Having a favourite subject, or even subjects, that you enjoy and are good at is a really good thing because it gives you a sense of enjoyment and achievement in your learning, which in turn boosts your confidence as a learner.

EXERCISE 1

My Subjects

Complete the table opposite by answering the questions in each of the boxes. You might have to do some research or ask your teacher/friends to help you with some of the questions e.g. What is this subject about?

My Subjects	What is it about?	Do I like it? Yes / No / Not Sure	Why?	What would make it easier?
Irish				
English				
Maths				
Science				
Business Studies				
CSPE				
SPHE				
History				
Geography				

EXERCISE 2

My favourite subjects

a. Write down your five favourite subjects.

(i) _____   (iv) _____

(ii) _____   (v) _____

(iii) _____

b. Write down the five subjects you find the easiest.

(i) _____   (iv) _____

(ii) _____   (v) _____

(iii) _____

c. What does this tell you?

_____

_____

_____

PAUSE AND REFLECT

1. What have you learned in this lesson?

_____

_____

2. How did you learn this?

_____

_____

3. How can you use what you learned in your schoolwork/study?

_____

_____

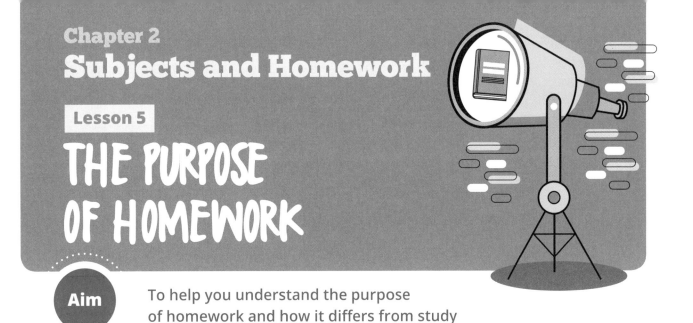

Chapter 2
Subjects and Homework

Lesson 5

THE PURPOSE OF HOMEWORK

Aim To help you understand the purpose of homework and how it differs from study

 Learning Point 1

Your volume of homework generally increases in secondary school. You will need to adapt to a longer day and more homework in the evenings. We will learn why we get homework and why it is important.

EXERCISE 1

Homework Q&A – Individual or Group Exercise

a. What is homework?

_____

b. Is homework important? Why?

_____

c. Who should monitor homework?

_____

d. How can we improve our learning from homework?

_____

e. Where and when do I record my homework?

_____

f. What do I do if I don't understand my homework?

_____

g. Making a good effort with homework involves what?

_____

Learning Point 2

Homework reinforces what was covered in class. Homework is an opportunity for you to review what was covered in class on your own and check to see if you understand what was done. The most important thing to realise now is that homework is PREPARATION FOR CLASS and is focused on understanding and study is PREPARATION FOR ASSESSMENTS and is focused on remembering.

What is Study? Word Box Exercise

Here is a list of activities you might be engaged in for your homework and study. Can you identify which activity you would normally do as homework and which one you would normally do as part of your study? If you can think of any other activities for either homework or study you can add them in at the end.

reviewing class work / taking notes / summarising / highlighting / answering questions / discussing / listening / writing / researching / revising / drawing / practising answers

Homework	Study

 EXERCISE **3**

What might your homework and study look like?

a. What is your favourite subject?

_____

b. Write down the typical homework you might get for this subject.

_____

_____

c. If you were to do some additional STUDY for this subject, what could it involve?

_____

_____

_____

EXERCISE **4**

Define homework and study
Complete the following sentences:

a. Homework is preparation for _____

and is focused on _____.

b. Study is preparation for _____

and is focused on _____.

PAUSE AND REFLECT

1. What have you learned in this lesson?

_____

_____

2. How did you learn this?

_____

_____

3. How can you use what you learned in your schoolwork/study?

_____

_____

_____

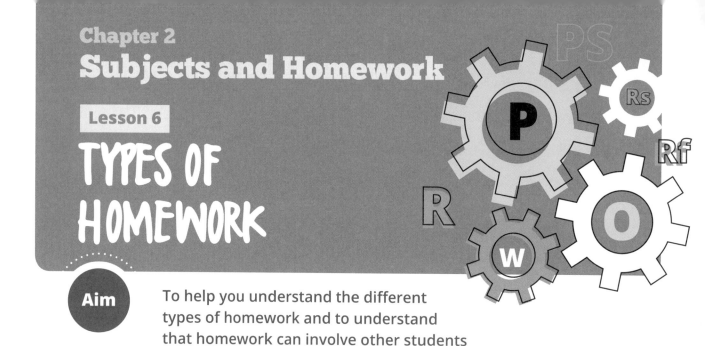

Chapter 2
Subjects and Homework

Lesson 6
TYPES OF HOMEWORK

Aim To help you understand the different types of homework and to understand that homework can involve other students

 Learning Point 1

You will encounter new types of homework in secondary school. Let's look at your subjects and the different types of homework you might be assigned.

 EXERCISE 1

Types of Homework – Matching Exercise

In the middle column write down an example of the homework you might get in the subject.

In the third column write down what TYPE of homework you have used as your example.

The codes are in the grid below. The first one is done for you.

Add more subjects if you wish. Your teacher may add more SUBJECTS or TYPES also.

Types of Homework

P Practice	**Rf** Reflecting	**O** Observing
R Reading	**W** Writing	**Re** Remembering
Rs Researching	**PS** Problem Solving	

Subject	Homework Example	Homework Types
Maths	Questions on Fractions	P – W – PS
English		
Irish		
French/ German		
Science		
Business		
Geography		
History		
Sports		
Music		
Woodwork		
Metalwork		
Home Economics		

 **Learning Point 2**

You might do homework every night, but you might also have homework that takes a few nights or a number of weeks to complete. You might also work alone or with others in a group. Let's interview our friends and see what homework experience we have so far.

 EXERCISE 2

An Interview!

Do you know how long homework might take and what is involved? Are we all the same when it comes to homework? Interview the person beside you by asking them the following questions to find out what their thoughts on homework are.

When finished, that person will then interview you!

a. What homework do you like best?

_____

b. What homework do you like least?

_____

c. How long do you spend doing your homework?

_____

d. What is the longest/shortest time you have spent on homework?

_____

e. Have you ever had group homework?   ☐ Yes ☐ No
   If yes, what did the group homework involve?

_____

_____

f. Do you prefer group homework or individual homework?

_____

g. Who might help you with group homework?

_____

h. What TYPES of homework could be done in a group?

_____

EXERCISE 3

a. Was your friend's experience of homework similar to yours?
☐ Yes ☐ No

Explain: _____

b. Did you enjoy talking to your friend about their homework experience? ☐ Yes ☐ No

Explain: _____

c. Did you learn anything by talking to your friend about homework? ☐ Yes ☐ No

Explain: _____

PAUSE AND REFLECT

1. What have you learned in this lesson?

_____
_____

2. How did you learn this?

_____
_____

3. How can you use what you learned in your schoolwork/study?

_____
_____

MENTAL NOTE

> **"The most effective way to do it, is to do it!"** – Amelia Earhart

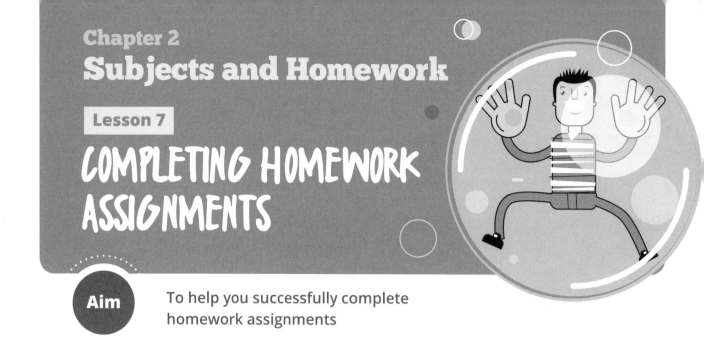

Chapter 2
Subjects and Homework

Lesson 7
COMPLETING HOMEWORK ASSIGNMENTS

Aim   To help you successfully complete homework assignments

 Learning Point 1

A key consideration for you in completing homework assignments is the physical space you have to work in. It is important to recognise any distractions and other barriers to completing tasks. Firstly you will explore some pictures to help you figure out what might be right and wrong in your work space.

 EXERCISE 1

a. Spot the Difference!

Look at the two pictures. There are a number of differences between the workspaces. Mark each of the differences with an X on the second picture.

b. How many differences did you notice?

EXERCISE 2

What's Your Opinion?

Now that you have examined the pictures and spotted the differences, write down your observations. Use the headings given to help you:

Item	What are your thoughts?
Phone	
Tidiness	
Earphones	
Window	
Curtains	
Fresh Air	
Desk	
Schoolbag	
The Bedroom	

EXERCISE 3

My space

a. What does your homework space look like?

_____

b. Could you make any changes to it?

_____

c. Are there other places you could do homework?

_____

d. What are the main distractions in your homework space right now?

_____

e. Any other thoughts on your homework space?

_____

 Learning Point 2

Try to be organised and structured in your approach to homework tasks. Do not rush homework or leave it undone. Try to understand the task and ask your teacher for feedback.

EXERCISE 4

Task Timeline

You are given the following homework task, 'Design a poster for bullying week.' Before you start you need to organise yourself by creating a timeline of all the things you might need to do, or actions. Here is a list of all the actions you need to do, however they are not in any order. Can you place them in the correct sequence on the template for the timeline?

Record homework	Read over and check content
Explore ideas	Identify what materials you need
Ask teacher questions	Consider options
Create poster	Ensure neat presentation
Decide on time needed	Check success criteria with teacher

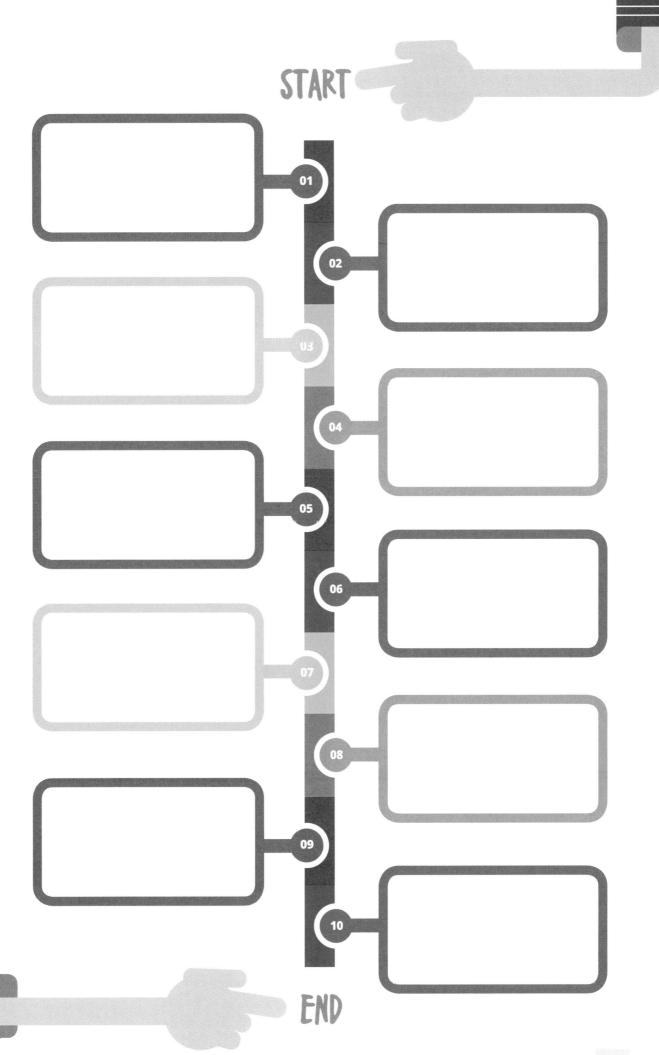

START

01

02

03

04

05

06

07

08

09

10

STEND

37

Learning Point 3

Top Five Tips for Homework:

1.

Establish a routine and commit to doing up to 2 hours' homework and revision each night in 1st year.

2.

Always do your homework first and then do your revision.

3.

Do your homework in a quiet place, no distractions, no social media. Homework takes much longer to do when you are distracted.

4.

Always attempt your homework. The correct answer is not the important thing, it is important that you attempt things and learn from your mistakes.

5.

It can help to have the telephone number of others in your class. If you missed something you can always contact them.

PAUSE AND REFLECT

1. What have you learned in this lesson?

_____

_____

2. How did you learn this?

_____

_____

3. How can you use what you learned in your schoolwork/study?

_____

_____

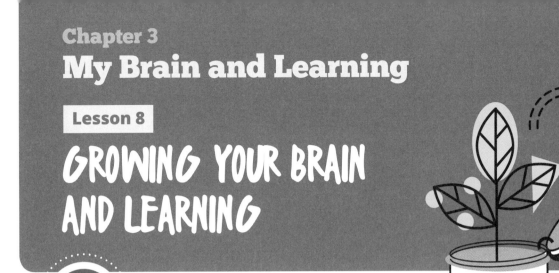

My Brain and Learning

Lesson 8

GROWING YOUR BRAIN AND LEARNING

Aim To help you understand that your brain can change and grow

Learning Point 1

Your brain remodels or remakes itself on an ongoing basis right throughout your life in response to your experiences and what you learn. Scientists now know that learning is biological, just like weightlifting. When you lift weights you exercise certain muscles, which grow. In the same way when you learn new things and have new experiences you remake or remodel parts of your brain and if you repeat these activities those parts of your brain become stronger. Learning is the process where we gain new information and skills and memory is the process where we retain that information over time. The more we practise, the stronger we are making those connections in our brains.

EXERCISE 1

The Brain and its Functions

What you do affects the growth of your brain. Struggling with certain skills helps your brain change and grow. If you stick at only what is easy your brain won't grow. Try answering these questions:

a. What things are you really good at doing?

b. What things do you want to be better at doing?

c. Who do you know that is good at something social or emotional (like helping others or being kind)?

d. Who do you know that is good at something physical or kinaesthetic (like playing sport or music or doing things with their hands)?

_____

e. Who do you know that is really good at something cognitive (thinking about things, school)?

_____

f. What have all these people done to be really good at these skills?

_____

g. What can you do to become much better at the things you really want to be good at doing?

_____

_____

h. Is it possible for you?

_____

i. So what do you now know?

_____

_____

_____

 Learning Point 2

Learning does not happen the first time you hear information or practise something. In fact, there are four Stages of Learning. Let's look at an example to explain each stage – riding a bike.

Stage 1: Before you get up on the bike you simply do not know what you do not know! You've never ridden a bike before. **Stage 2:** Once you get on the saddle you quickly begin to realise what you do not know. This is when frustration can set in, or fear in case you're going to fall. This frustration or fear could cause you to give up. But most of us try to work through these feelings and continue. **Stage 3:** Once you have been shown how to keep your balance, hold the handlebars, pedal, and use the brakes, you begin to cycle, but with great care and concentration. You want/need to get it right. The final stage is where your confidence kicks in.
Stage 4: Through practice cycling becomes second nature to you and you don't even need to think about it anymore.

Matching!

Match the stages to the feelings expressed in the pictures below by placing the correct number in each circle. Think about how you might feel if it was you.

Stage 1: 'I don't know! And I don't know what I don't know!'

Stage 2: 'I know that I don't know.'

Stage 3: 'I know, but I have to think about it constantly.'

Stage 4: 'I know, and I can do it without thinking!'

Happy / Oblivious

Delighted/ Proud

Frustrated / Confused

Focused / Alert

EXERCISE 3

Learning is Fun and Frustrating!

Sometimes you might expect to go from Stage 1 to Stage 4, skipping the confusion and frustration associated with the middle steps. This would be easy for us all! But learning can be tricky and you must stick with it, even when it is hard or frustrating.

Think about the things you learn – in school, at home, in life in general. It could be learning to play a sport or instrument, learning a poem off by heart, baking a cake or how to take care of a pet, learning the alphabet or even how to click your fingers! List five things you have learned so far in life:

(i) _____

(ii) _____

(iii) _____

(iv) _____

(v) _____

My Learning

Answer the following:

a. Have you ever felt frustrated when learning something new?
   ☐ Yes ☐ No

b. What did you do?

   _____

   _____

   _____

c. What stage of learning might make you most frustrated?

   _____

d. What stage might give you confidence?

   _____

EXERCISE 4   **Read the story and answer the questions below.**

Eva goes to horse riding lessons. She began at 9 years old, she is 14 now. Before she went to lessons Eva thought horse riding looked like great fun. She wished she could just sit on the horse's back and gallop through the fields with the wind in her hair.

Eva went to her first day of riding class and sat on a horse for the first time. She was walked over to a stable. The instructor began by showing her how to open the door, how to enter a stable, what side of the horse was safest, how to put on a saddle, how to put on the reins and much more. She told Eva the names of all the straps, leathers and equipment. There were a lot of straps, the leather saddle and the stirrups for her feet had to be adjusted, so too did the reins. Eva's head was spinning. She was confused and wondering if this was right for her after all.

Next, she was told to follow the instructor and horse into the arena for the riding lesson. Eva was helped onto her horse, Saffron. The stirrups had to be adjusted again. Eva felt very high up, far from the safety of the ground. She had earlier been given a whip, a helmet and a back protector. Saffron started to walk after the other horses in the arena and ignored Eva when she pulled gently on the reins to try to stop her. The instructor began shouting commands to the class, 'sit up', 'heels down', 'whip in your right hand', 'bend your elbows', 'bend your knees'.

Eva's first lesson wasn't as thrilling as she had imagined. Saffron was stubborn and did not like to halt or stop when the reins were pulled too hard. Eva had to learn quickly to apply just enough pressure but to use her legs even more than her reins. A good rider will have great influence over their horse with their legs, not just their reins. Eva managed to trot a little in the first lesson but she ached afterwards as she struggled to find a rhythm with Saffron. The instructor called 'up, down, up, down, up, down.' Eva tried hard but only for a second did she manage to fall into her horse's pace. The rest of the time she was bumped up and down on the horse's back and she was very uncomfortable.

a. List three things Eva might have been thinking before she went for her first lesson.

(i) _____

(ii) _____

(iii) _____

b. On the day of the lesson how might Eva have felt?

_____

c. When Eva was shown the horse in the stable with all the equipment, what did she think?

_____

d. (i) Do you think Eva was nervous? ☐ **Yes** ☐ **No**

(ii) When might she have been nervous?

_____

e. Eva had second thoughts. What caused this?

_____

f. Was Eva happy after the first lesson? ☐ **Yes** ☐ **No**

g. What options did Eva have after the first lesson?

_____

h. What do you think Eva should do? Quit, try one more time, commit to a few lessons, practise, read up on horses, watch clips on horse riding, do nothing?

_____

_____

PAUSE AND REFLECT

1. What have you learned in this lesson?

_____

_____

2. How did you learn this?

_____

_____

3. How can you use what you learned in your schoolwork/study?

_____

_____

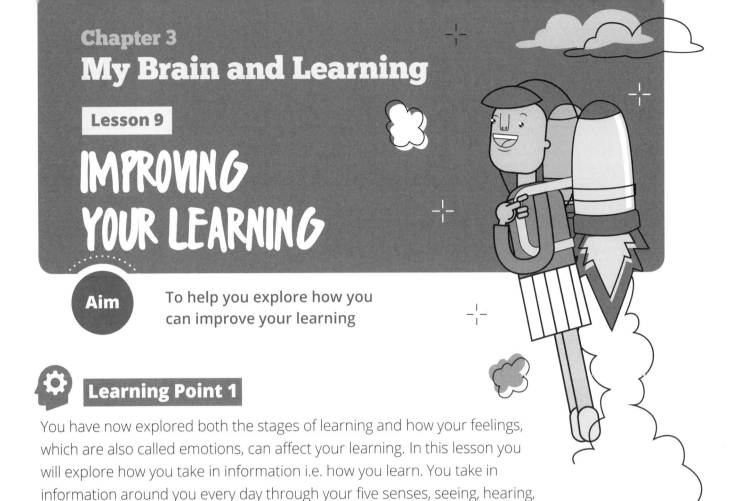

Chapter 3

My Brain and Learning

Lesson 9

IMPROVING YOUR LEARNING

Aim To help you explore how you can improve your learning

Learning Point 1

You have now explored both the stages of learning and how your feelings, which are also called emotions, can affect your learning. In this lesson you will explore how you take in information i.e. how you learn. You take in information around you every day through your five senses, seeing, hearing, touch, taste and smell. In your learning at school you tend to rely primarily on three of these senses:

(i) Sight, which is called visual learning

(ii) Hearing, which is called auditory learning

(iii) Touch, which is called kinaesthetic learning.

Whilst you use all your senses, students tend to have a preference for how they learn best or simply which is the best way for them to take in information.

EXERCISE 1

Sensory learning

Do you know which sense you have a preference for? Answer the following questions by circling the correct one for you.

a. When I get a new phone or tablet, I:

 (a) Read the instructions first

 (b) Listen to an explanation from someone who has used it before

 (c) Go ahead and have a go, I can figure it out as I use it

b. When I need directions, I usually:

 (a) Look at a map

 (b) Ask for spoken directions

 (c) Follow my nose and maybe use a compass

c. When I'm explaining how to do something, I tend to say:

- **(a)** Watch how I do it
- **(b)** Listen to me explain
- **(c)** You have a go

d. When I go shopping for clothes, I tend to:

- **(a)** Imagine what they would look like on
- **(b)** Discuss them with the shop staff
- **(c)** Try them on and test them out

e. When I am learning something new, I:

- **(a)** Watch what the teacher is doing
- **(b)** Talk through with the teacher exactly what I'm supposed to do
- **(c)** Give it a try myself and work it out as I go

f. If I am choosing food from a menu, I tend to:

- **(a)** Imagine what the food will look like
- **(b)** Talk through the options in my head or with my companion
- **(c)** Imagine what the food will taste like

g. When I listen to a band, I can't help:

- **(a)** Watching the band members and other people in the audience
- **(b)** Listening to the lyrics and the beats
- **(c)** Moving in time with the music

h. When I concentrate, I most often:

- **(a)** Focus on the words or the pictures in front of me
- **(b)** Discuss any problems and possible solutions in my head
- **(c)** Move around a lot, fiddle with pens and pencils and touch things

i. My first memory is of:

- **(a)** Looking at something
- **(b)** Being spoken to
- **(c)** Doing something

j. When I am anxious, I:

- **(a)** Visualise the worst case scenarios
- **(b)** Talk over in my head what worries me most
- **(c)** Can't sit still, fiddle and move around constantly

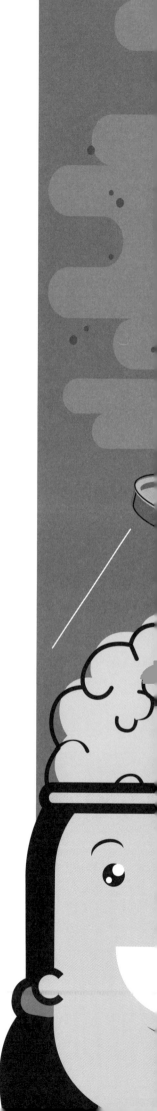

k. I feel especially connected to other people because of:

   (a) How they look

   (b) What they say to me

   (c) How they make me feel

l. When I have to revise for an exam, I generally:

   (a) Write lots of revision notes and diagrams

   (b) Talk over my notes, alone or with other people

   (c) Imagine carrying out the action

m. I really love:

   (a) Watching films, photography, looking at art or people watching

   (b) Listening to music, the radio or talking to friends

   (c) Taking part in sporting activities, eating good food or dancing

n. Most of my free time is spent:

   (a) Watching television

   (b) Talking to friends

   (c) Doing physical activity or making things

o. I first notice how people:

   (a) Look and dress

   (b) Sound and speak

   (c) Stand and move

p. If I am angry, I tend to:

   (a) Keep replaying in my mind what it is that has upset me

   (b) Raise my voice and tell people how I feel

   (c) Stamp about, slam doors and physically demonstrate my anger

q. I find it easiest to remember:

   (a) Faces

   (b) Names

   (c) Things I have done

r. I think that you can tell if someone is lying if:

   (a) They avoid looking at you

   (b) Their voice changes

   (c) They give you funny vibes

s. I remember things best by:

(a) Writing notes or keeping printed details

(b) Saying them aloud or repeating words and key points in my head

(c) Doing and practising the activity or imagining it being done

t. I tend to say:

(a) I see what you mean

(b) I hear what you are saying

(c) I know how you feel.

Now add up how many A's, B's and C's you selected as answers to the questions above.

A's

B's

C's

If you chose mostly A's you have a **VISUAL** learning style. If you chose mostly B's you have an **AUDITORY** learning style. If you chose mostly C's you have a **KINAESTHETIC** learning style.

Some people find that their learning style is a blend of two or three styles.

Your learning style

a. From the previous exercise what is your preferred learning style?

b. Describe in your own words what you think this means about how you learn.

EXERCISE 3

Tips for learning

Here is a list of tips for each learning style. Can you match each set of tips with the correct learning style? Write the correct style in at the top of the column.

AUDITORY

VISUAL

KINAESTHETIC

Use highlighter for main ideas and keywords	Write vocabulary words on an index card and walk around whilst reciting them.	Review vocabulary and notes by reading them out loud to yourself.
Pay attention to graphs/ pictures/ charts.	Try to act out words or events with simple gestures that will help you remember them.	Verbalise things you want to remember.
When listening to the teacher always look at them.	Use a highlighter pen for main ideas in your textbook and notes to allow your hand to keep moving.	Read aloud whenever possible.
Sit close to the front of the classroom so you have a clear view of the board and the teacher.	Try studying in different positions and change positions frequently.	Study with a friend so you can discuss and hear the information.
Use graphic note taking methods such as mind mapping and visual aids.	Take frequent short breaks and do something that involves light activity.	Use familiar songs to help you memorise details by substituting the original words.
Preview a chapter before reading it by looking at the titles, introduction, subtopics, keywords and summary.	Whenever possible, "do" your assignments and projects in an active way.	Ask your teacher to repeat something, especially if you don't understand it.

EXERCISE 4

Your own tips

Looking back at your preferred learning style, which can be a combination of two, write down what four tips you will use in your learning going forward.

(i) _____

_____

(ii) _____

_____

(iii) _____

_____

(iv) _____

PAUSE AND REFLECT

1. What have you learned in this lesson?

_____

_____

2. How did you learn this?

_____

_____

3. How can you use what you learned in your schoolwork/study?

_____

_____

MENTAL NOTE

"We don't grow when things are easy,
we grow when we face challenges." – Joyce Meyer

Chapter 3
My Brain and Learning

Lesson 10

PAIRED AND GROUP LEARNING

Aim   To explore group working

 Learning Point 1 Two heads are better than one

Another way of reinforcing your learning is when you share what you have learned with others. This builds your understanding of the topic along with reinforcing those connections in your brain, aiding your long-term memory. Sometimes when the concept might be new or difficult, working it out with a partner can also make the learning easier, simply by being able to discuss it.

 Two heads are better than one

The following exercise is taken from your English course. Newspaper headlines can be either informative or entertaining. From the following list of newspaper headlines choose which ones are informative and which ones are entertaining.

Complete the exercise first on your own and when completed turn to your partner to see what answers they got. After each headline circle either I for Informative or E for Entertaining.

		My Answer	My Partner's Answer
a.	(i) Wild Dog Snatches Tot	I / E	I / E
	(ii) Dingo Carries Baby Away	I / E	I / E
	(iii) Adjudicator Accidentally Posts Results of Miss Cobra Pageant	I / E	I / E
	(iv) Turkey in Soup for Tweeting Picture of New Miss Cobra	I / E	I / E
	(v) Animal Rights Campaigners Open Gates in Zoo	I / E	I / E

		My Answer	My Partner's Answer
(vi)	Loonies Let Wild Beasts Loose		
(vii)	Humans Must Respect Wild Creatures - Animal Expert	I / E	I / E
(viii)	Egg-head Lashes Zoo Visitors	I / E	I / E
(ix)	Astronomy Photographer of the Year	I / E	I / E
(x)	Star Snapper Hits the Heights	I / E	I / E
(adapted from Spirals, New Junior Cycle English, EDCO, Campion et al., 2014)		I / E	I / E

b. **(i)** Discuss with your partner why you chose each answer.

(ii) Were you able to clearly explain your answers to your partner? ☐ Yes ☐ No

(iii) Do you think having to explain your answers will help you remember the exercise more? ☐ Yes ☐ No

(iv) Why do you think this is the case?

_____

_____

_____

_____

 **Learning Point 2**

What a Cooperative Group might look like

Group learning may be new for you or you might already know that working together can be tricky. Teamwork is a key life skill, one that you begin to work on both in school and in other areas of life. You may prefer working alone, which isn't a problem. However, you still need to engage in group activities. Each group has different roles that you may step into and out of depending on the group and the group task. The different roles may play to your strengths, or perhaps can be a challenge for you. Cooperative groups (groups that work together on a common task) generally have the following roles:

Cooperative Groups

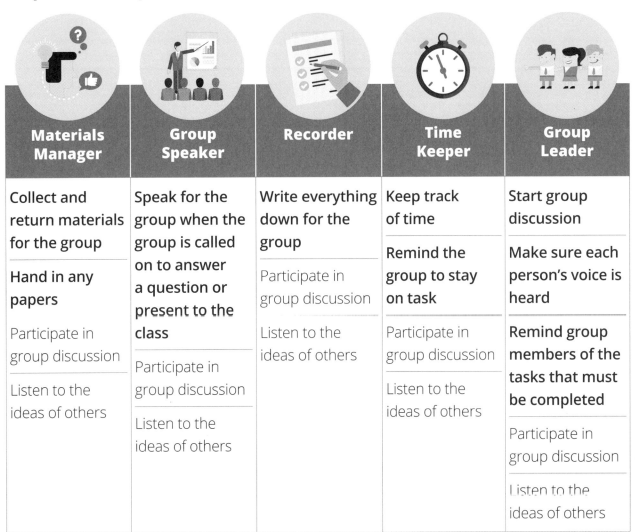

Materials Manager	Group Speaker	Recorder	Time Keeper	Group Leader
Collect and return materials for the group	Speak for the group when the group is called on to answer a question or present to the class	Write everything down for the group	Keep track of time	Start group discussion
Hand in any papers		Participate in group discussion	Remind the group to stay on task	Make sure each person's voice is heard
Participate in group discussion	Participate in group discussion	Listen to the ideas of others	Participate in group discussion	Remind group members of the tasks that must be completed
Listen to the ideas of others	Listen to the ideas of others		Listen to the ideas of others	Participate in group discussion
				Listen to the ideas of others

 EXERCISE 2 **Group Forming**

→ Your teacher will sort you into groups. There are 5 roles which must be assigned – Materials Manager, Speaker, Recorder, Time Keeper and Group Leader.

→ As a group you must decide on the allocation of the roles.

→ Your group task is to organise a year group cleanup for everybody as part of your school's Green Flag.

→ You only have five minutes to come up with suggestions to give back to the class.

→ You can write your suggestions on a separate sheet of paper.

→ Once your group is sorted and roles assigned, everybody should answer the following questions:

a. How do you feel about your role?

b. Would you have liked to try a different role?　☐ Yes ☐ No

c. How did your group decide what roles were assigned to people?

_____

_____

d. Did you think the deciding was fair? ☐ Yes ☐ No

e. Were some people quieter than others? ☐ Yes ☐ No

f. Were some people more vocal than others? ☐ Yes ☐ No

g. Did everybody get to share their thoughts? ☐ Yes ☐ No

h. Do you think working in groups is a good thing? ☐ Yes ☐ No

i. Do you prefer to work alone? ☐ Yes ☐ No

j. What might be the benefits of group work?

_____

_____

 Learning Point 3 Group Development Stages

Groups generally go through 5 key stages of development, Forming, Storming, Norming, Performing and Adjourning. The meaning of these terms can be seen in this graphic:

Cooperative Groups

Norming

People begin to see themselves as part of the group and realise that to achieve their task they need to accept the opinions of others.

Storming

Each person still sees themselves as individuals and may resent the opinions of others. They don't feel part of a group yet.

Forming

Everybody introduces themselves to each other, very formal and ground rules for behaviour are created.

Adjourning

When the task is finished the group reflects on what they have achieved together.

Performing

The group works well together and everybody is on task and working in their assigned role.

As you can see some argument and disagreement is part of the process and some may be better equipped to deal with this. Ultimately groups will make decisions that may require a majority vote if differences persist; accepting this vote if you are the minority can be difficult. Groups can go through this phase very quickly or very slowly, depending on the task, how well they know each other already, how often they meet etc.

EXERCISE 3

Group Reflection

Reflecting on your previous task try and answer the following questions.

a. Did any disagreement arise? ☐ **Yes** ☐ **No**.

b. How did you feel about it?

_____

_____

c. How was agreement reached?

_____

_____

d. Could you suggest another way of reaching agreement?

_____

_____

EXERCISE 4

Group Task

As previously stated, for some, group learning may be new and it can be tricky! Teamwork is a key life skill, one you will use in all areas of your life, school, home, work, with friends, sports etc. You will always work with groups at some stage so it is important to know how to do so effectively. You have 10 minutes to try and answer as many riddles here as you can. You will do it first on your own, then with your learning partner and then finally in a group. Write your individual answer on line **(i)**, your learning partner's answer on line **(ii)**, and the group's answer on line **(iii)** for each one.

a. What has hands but cannot clap?

(i) _____

(ii) _____

(iii) _____

b. What starts with the letter "t", is filled with "t" and ends in "t"?

(i) _____

(ii) _____

(iii) _____

c. Which weighs more, a pound of feathers or a pound of bricks?

(i) _____

(ii) _____

(iii) _____

d. How many months have 28 days?

(i) _____

(ii) _____

(iii) _____

e. Name four days of the week that start with the letter "t".

(i) _____

(ii) _____

(iii) _____

f. What goes around and around the wood but never goes into the wood?

(i) _____

(ii) _____

(iii) _____

g. Two mothers and two daughters went out to eat, everyone ate one burger, yet only three burgers were eaten in all. How is this possible?

(i) _____

(ii) _____

(iii) _____

h. A man was outside taking a walk, when it started to rain. The man didn't have an umbrella and he wasn't wearing a hat.
His clothes got soaked, yet not a single hair on his head got wet. How could this happen?

(i) _____

(ii) _____

(iii) _____

i. A boy was rushed to the hospital emergency room. The ER doctor saw the boy and said, "I cannot operate on this boy. He is my son." But the doctor was not the boy's father. How could that be?

(i) _____

(ii) _____

(iii) _____

j. If there are 3 apples and you take away 2, how many do you have?

(i) _____

(ii) _____

(iii) _____

k. I am an odd number. Take away one letter and I become even. What number am I?

(i) _____

(ii) _____

(iii) _____

l. What never asks questions but is often answered?

(i) _____

(ii) _____

(iii) _____

m. What belongs to you but other people use it more than you?

(i) _____

(ii) _____

(iii) _____

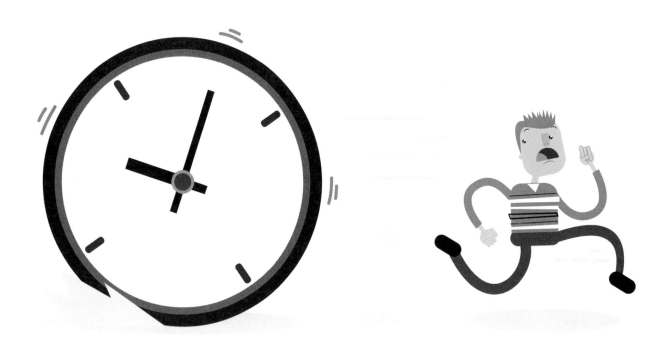

EXERCISE 5

a. How many did you get working on your own?

SCORE

b. How many did you get working with your learning partner?

SCORE

c. How many did you get working in groups?

SCORE

d. Which was the easiest way of answering the riddles: individually, in pairs or in groups?

_____

_____

Sometimes when you are learning or studying it is easier when you work with others!

PAUSE AND REFLECT

1. What have you learned in this lesson?

_____

_____

2. How did you learn this?

_____

_____

3. How can you use what you learned in your schoolwork/study?

_____

_____

Lesson 11

BEHAVIOURS FOR LEARNING

Aim To explore how rules can help you with your learning

 Learning Point 1

Whatever you call them, rules are simply guidelines to help you feel safe and secure. Rules promote respect and allow you to be part of the school community. You should contribute to making your class safe and secure for everybody to be able to enjoy learning.

 EXERCISE 1 Proper Behaviour!

Here is a list of different types of behaviours. Read through each one and answer whether you think it would help learning take place or not in the classroom. Give a reason for each of your answers.

a. Everybody talking at the same time? ☐ Yes ☐ No

   Reason:

   _____

   _____

b. Students getting up and walking around the classroom when you are trying to work? ☐ Yes ☐ No

   Reason:

   _____

   _____

c. Other students jumping in with their answers all the time?
   ☐ Yes ☐ No

   Reason:

   _____

   _____

d. Nobody listening to the teacher or each other? ☐ Yes ☐ No

   Reason:

   _____

EXERCISE 2 — Rules for Learning – rate yourself

As you have seen from the previous exercise there are some very simple things you can do in class which help you learn. Sometimes these are called the 3 rules for class, which are

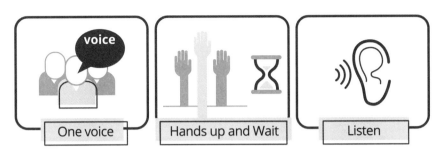

One voice | Hands up and Wait | Listen

Out of 10, rate your adherence to the 3 rules for class. Can you explain each score you give?

Only one
person
speaking at a
time

One Voice ◯

Explain:

_____

_____

Taking
turns to ask
questions,
talk or get
the teacher's
attention

Hands Up and Wait ◯

Explain:

_____

_____

Being a good
listener,
to other
students and
to teachers

Listen ◯

Explain:

_____

_____

My Total ◯

What one thing could you do which would have greatest impact on your learning?

_____

_____

EXERCISE 3   Benefits of Good Behaviour!

What images BEST illustrate the benefits of good behaviour?
Tick as many as you wish.

 PAUSE AND REFLECT

1. What have you learned in this lesson?

_____

_____

2. How did you learn this?

_____

_____

3. How can you use what you learned in your schoolwork/study?

_____

_____

62

Chapter 4
Behaviours for Learning

Lesson 12

SKILLS AND ATTITUDES

Aim To introduce you to the behaviours for learning

Learning Point 1

Let's look at some of the skills and attitudes that can help you become a more effective learner. Here are a few definitions you may need to know.

A skill is something that you do well. By doing something regularly you become good at it, it is something you can say you are skilled at.

An attitude is your outlook or approach to something. You can decide to approach your work in a positive way, which means that you are willing to put in the extra effort that may be needed to succeed.

Behaviour is the way you act and conduct yourself towards others and your work. So doing something regularly with a particular attitude becomes a behaviour.

Here you will explore some of the skills and behaviours which can help you in becoming a more effective student. These are referred to as the skills and behaviours for learning.

EXERCISE 1

Understanding Skills and Behaviours for Learning

Here is a list of definitions for each key skill and behaviour for learning; can you write the skill and behaviour beside its correct definition?

Organised, Punctual, Co-operative, Attentive, Hardworking, Persistent, Thoughtful, Optimistic

Thinking of others and their feelings	
Doing my best work	
Having all I need for class	
Finding the best in every situation	
Concentrating on my learning	
Being on time for all classes	
Helping others in a positive way	
Working hard even when the going gets though	

EXERCISE 2

Match each of the key skills and behaviours for learning with the correct image.

EXERCISE 3 — When Do I Display These Skills and Behaviours?

Having looked at some of the skills and behaviours of effective learners, can you think of situations or examples of where they might be important? **Write as many as you can for each skill/attitude.**

a. **Attentive:** _____

b. **Co-operative:** _____

c. **Hardworking:** _____

d. **Punctual:** _____

e. **Organised:** _____

f. **Persistent:** _____

g. **Optimistic:** _____

h. **Thoughtful:** _____

 Learning Point 2

You are the key to your own success in learning, therefore it is important that you make the effort to behave in a way that will help you learn faster, better, smarter.

 PAUSE AND REFLECT

1. What have you learned in this lesson?

_____

_____

2. How did you learn this?

_____

_____

3. How can you use what you learned in your schoolwork/study?

_____

_____

 MENTAL NOTE

"Teachers open the door but you must enter by yourself." – Chinese proverb

Chapter 4
Behaviours for Learning

Lesson 13

KEY SKILLS FOR JUNIOR CYCLE

Aim To make you aware of the key skills that you will develop during the Junior Cycle

 Learning Point 1

The new Junior Cycle key skills help you develop the knowledge, skills and attitudes to face the many challenges in today's world. They also help you in learning how to learn and to take responsibility for your own learning. As you develop each of the key skills in an integrated way you will also become a better learner.

 EXERCISE 1

Junior Cycle Key Skills

Here is the list of key skills that the Department of Education and Skills wish all students to develop during their time in school. Try and match the various definitions of the skills on the next page with the right key skill.

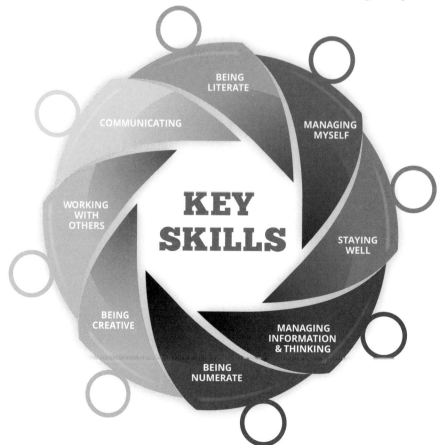

a Developing my understanding and enjoyment of words and language

→ Reading for enjoyment and with critical understanding

→ Writing for different purposes

→ Expressing ideas clearly and accurately

→ Developing my spoken language

→ Exploring and creating a variety of texts, including multi-modal texts.

b Using language

→ Using numbers

→ Listening and expressing myself

→ Performing and presenting

→ Discussing and debating

→ Using digital technology to communicate.

c Being healthy and physically active

→ Being social

→ Being safe

→ Being spiritual

→ Being confident

→ Being positive about learning

→ Being responsible, safe and ethical in using digital technology.

d Knowing myself

→ Making considered decisions

→ Setting and achieving personal goals

→ Being able to reflect on my own learning

→ Using digital technology to manage myself and my learning.

e Being curious

→ Gathering, recording, organising and evaluating information and data

→ Thinking creatively and critically

→ Reflecting on and evaluating my learning

→ Using digital technology to access, manage and share content.

f Imagining

→ Exploring options and alternatives

→ Implementing ideas and taking action

→ Learning creatively

→ Stimulating creativity using digital technology.

g Developing good relationships and dealing with conflict

→ Co-operating

→ Respecting difference

→ Contributing to making the world a better place

→ Learning with others

→ Working with others through digital technology.

h Expressing ideas mathematically

→ Estimating, predicting and calculating

→ Developing a positive disposition towards investigating, reasoning and problem solving

→ Seeing patterns, trends and relationships

→ Gathering, interpreting and representing data

→ Using digital technology to develop numeracy skills and understanding.

EXERCISE 2

Key Skills and Subjects

For each skill, try and identify the subject in which you think you will develop this key skill. Write the subjects in each square beside the key skill.

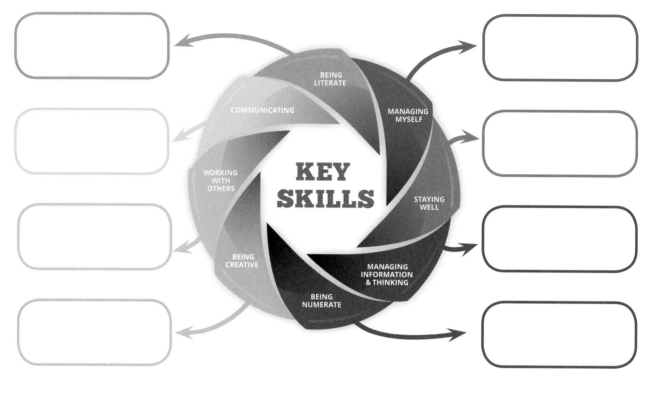

a. How many subjects on average did you have for each skill?

b. What does this tell you?

   (i)

   (ii)

Lesson 14

SKILLS FOR LEARNING - LISTENING 1

Aim To explore the essential skill of listening

Learning Point 1

Listening is a key life skill and one we must all master if we want to succeed both in school and in life.

In this busy, noisy world sometimes we forget how important the skill of listening actually is, even if it means listening to something which we might not necessarily find interesting.

EXERCISE 1

Me as a listener

a. On a scale of 1-10, where 1 is poor and 10 is excellent, how would you rate your ability to listen?

| 1 | 2 | 3 | 4 | 5 | 6 | 7 | 8 | 9 | 10 |

b. Give a reason for your answer:

_____

_____

_____

_____

c. Now read the following questions and score yourself from 1 to 5 for each statement, where

1 strongly disagree
2 disagree
3 neither agree nor disagree
4 agree
5 strongly agree

I speak and listen respectfully to each person.	
I let others finish what they are trying to say, and if they hesitate I encourage them to go on.	
I never daydream or think about other things when listening to others.	
I don't text or mess around with my mobile phone when others are speaking.	
I don't have a hard time paying attention to boring people.	
I listen to others' feedback all the time.	
I don't stop listening to a speaker even when I think he or she has nothing interesting to say.	
I do not expend a lot of energy when listening to others.	
My body language is consistent with my words. For example, if I ask 'How are you getting on?' then I listen to the response and don't look ready to rush off.	

If you scored

→ **34-40** you are an excellent listener

→ **28-33** you are quite good at listening when interested

→ **Lower than 28** you might want to look at developing your listening skills

Did your results surprise you in any way? ☐ Yes ☐ No
Why?

_____

_____

_____

What listening to each other, looks and sounds like

Did you ever think about what listening looks and sounds like? Well here's your chance. Try and complete this T list, where you first imagine what listening looks and sounds like and then write down your answers .

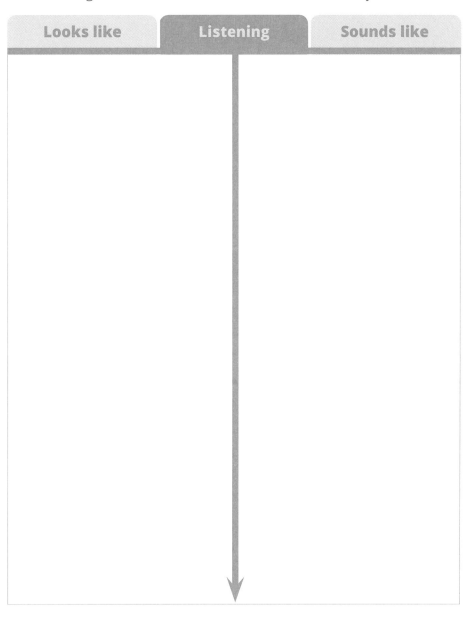

Looks like	Listening	Sounds like

Did anyone else have something different to what you had on your list? If so, you can add it in now.

_____

_____

_____

_____

EXERCISE 3

Improving my listening

a. Now that you have looked at what listening might look and sound like, how would you rate your ability to listen on the scale of 1 -10?

| 1 | 2 | 3 | 4 | 5 | 6 | 7 | 8 | 9 | 10 |

b. Has it changed? ☐ Yes ☐ No

c. What, if anything, has changed?

_____

_____

d. List three things that you think you can do to improve yourself as a listener.

(i) _____

(ii) _____

(iii) _____

PAUSE AND REFLECT

1. What have you learned in this lesson?

_____

_____

2. How did you learn this?

_____

_____

3. How can you use what you learned in your schoolwork/study?

_____

_____

Chapter 5
Managing Information: Listening

Lesson 15

SKILLS FOR LEARNING - LISTENING 2

Aim

To explore the essential skill of listening

Learning Point 1

Let's begin to apply what you learned in your previous lesson in the classroom.

EXERCISE 1

Listening to Teachers

Look at the following picture:

Answer the following questions:

a. Who is listening? How do you know?

_____

b. Who is not listening? How do you know?

_____

c. Why do people listen?

_____

d. Why do people not listen?

_____

e. What might the teacher say to those not listening?

_____

f. What might the teacher be feeling?

_____

g. What might the students who are listening be feeling?

_____

h. What might the non-listening students be feeling?

_____

Listening with purpose
Organise into pairs.

One student is A and the other B. Students sit back to back.
Student A reads the poem from the English course, with Student
B paying attention. When Student A is finished they ask Student B
the questions that follow to see how well Student B was listening.
Student A marks all the correct answers.
Student B keeps their book closed and doesn't look at the poem.

The students then swap roles, with Student B reading a section
of the Science course on Life. Make sure Student A has their
book closed.

Part a Student A:

Winter Playground by Jenny Craig

In the cold winter sunshine
The children stand against the wall.
They look like washing on a line.

Neat red coat, stripey mitts,
Narrow green tights with a hole in the knee.
Still and stiff, frozen in a row.

Across the playground
Three boys are chasing a ball.
A little dog barks through the fence.

A skipping rope curves-
'One I love, two I loathe....'
As the girls hop and jump.

The teacher stalks, eyes darting,
Scattering marbles in his way,
Keeping a look-out for TROUBLE.

(Spirals, New Junior Cycle English 1st Year,
Edco, Campion et al., 2016)

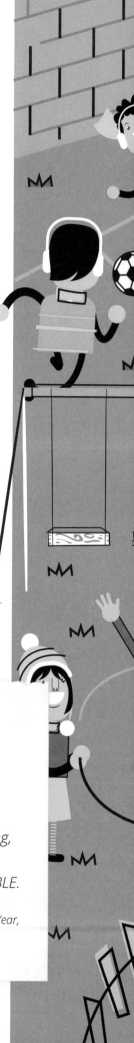

Questions:

	Correct	
	Yes	No
a. Who wrote the poem?		
b. Where were the children standing?		
c. How many boys were chasing the ball?		
d. How big was the dog?		
e. What was the teacher doing?		

Part b Student B:

Defining Life

Biology is the study of life. Every living thing is called an organism.
There are seven common features that help identify a living thing.
Each organism demonstrates all of the following characteristics of life.

1. Nutrition
2. Respiration
3. Excretion
4. Growth

5. Reproduction
6. Movement
7. Response

(Catalyst Junior Cycle Science, Educate.ie, Dundon et al., 2016)

Questions:

	Correct	
	Yes	No
a. What is the study of life called?		
b. What is the name for every living thing?		
c. What do you call a feature that helps identify a living thing?		
d. How many common characteristics are there?		
e. Name three of the characteristics.		
(i)		
(ii)		
(iii)		

EXERCISE 3

Tips for listening

Organise into pairs.

Match each of the following explanations with the correct tip.

The tips!

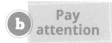 **a** Respond appropriately    **b** Pay attention    **c** Don't jump in   **d** Show that you're listening

Look at the speaker directly. Notice the speaker's body language as well as what they are actually saying.   ○

Use your own body language and gestures to convey your attention. Nod occasionally. Smile and use other facial expressions. If on a one-to-one encourage the speaker to continue with small verbal comments like yes, and uh huh.   ○

Interrupting is a waste of time. Allow the speaker to finish each point before asking questions.   ○

Treat the other person in a way that you think he or she would want to be treated.   ○

One final tip for you when trying to focus in class:

If you're finding it particularly difficult to concentrate on what someone is saying, try repeating their words mentally as they speak – this will reinforce their message and help you stay focused.

PAUSE AND REFLECT

1. What have you learned in this lesson?

_____

_____

2. How did you learn this?

_____

_____

3. How can you use what you learned in your schoolwork/study?

_____

MENTAL NOTE

"The dictionary is the only place where success comes before work." – Mark Twain

Chapter 6

Managing Information: Reading

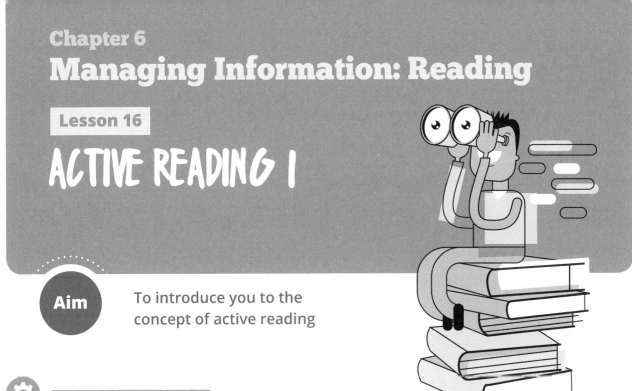

ACTIVE READING 1

Aim To introduce you to the concept of active reading

Learning Point 1

One of the identified key skills for the Junior Cycle that you are required to develop is called managing information and learning. This key skill helps you gradually improve your ability to interpret, to organise and to apply information that you come across in your learning. These next chapters will assist you in both.

Learning Point 2

As part of developing your managing information and learning skills you will explore ways in which you can improve your reading skills.

We can do a lot when we read, or not very much! Have you ever read something and realised at the end that you don't remember half of what you read? Maybe a text message, a page of a book or post?

Passive reading is when we are not really thinking about the content of the text at all. We merely skim over it, do not take it in or question it as we go along.

Active reading means that you are reading with a purpose, taking it in and maybe stopping to think about ideas as you read them. You might take notes, or ask questions as you go along.

Becoming an active reader takes practice. In these two lessons on active reading you will explore some simple techniques which will assist in reading and gaining a better understanding of what is going on in text.

A technique is a way of carrying out a particular task. Having gone through the various simple techniques here on active reading you can decide to adapt them to different types of text that you come across in your learning.

For today you will do a little practice on being aware while reading a text. Here are some simple steps to bring your awareness to your reading.

- Scan the text to get a general understanding of the ideas and structure. (Scan means to quickly read over without trying to read single words).

- Take note of any charts or pictures that add meaning to the text.

- Read through from beginning to end.

- Now highlight the words which carry the most meaning and any new words you have come across.

EXERCISE 1

Bringing awareness to text

For the text that follows on the Danish father and his son, apply the steps above and then complete the table that follows.

> ### *Danish father and son team up on homework and turn in a German warplane*
>
> When Daniel Rom Kristiansen, a 14-year-old student in northern Denmark, was given homework on World War II, his father had a jokey suggestion.
>
> Family legend had it that a plane crashed not far from their farm in 1944. "Go out and find the plane," the father, Klaus Kristiansen, suggested.
>
> Much to his surprise, Daniel did.
>
> What began as a good-natured attempt by a man to make history come alive for his son turned into headline-grabbing news this week when Daniel, aided by Mr. Kristiansen, discovered the wreckage of a German warplane, along with the remains of a man who might have been its pilot.
>
> After the discovery Monday, forensics police officers arrived to secure the site, along with bomb disposal experts and a representative from the German Embassy. Soon, the Danish news media descended on the farm, in the remote town of Birkelse in the north of the Jutland peninsula.
>
> Mr. Kristiansen told the Danish newspaper Politiken that his grandfather, who had lived on the farm, had told him years ago about the crash. But in 40 years of ploughing the fields, Mr. Kristiansen had seen no sign of the plane.
>
> After Daniel reacted enthusiastically to his fanciful challenge, Mr. Kristiansen said, he joined the boy in the field, armed with a metal detector — and more than a little scepticism.
>
> When the detector suddenly sounded, they started digging and found metal fragments, Mr. Kristiansen told Politiken. As their excitement mounted, they borrowed a mechanical excavator from a neighbour and dug about 16 feet into the ground.

He said they were amazed to find buried a machine gun part, the remnants of an engine, a fighter pilot's uniform, bones, a crew member's ID and a wallet holding coins and a condom.

"The plane had crashed into thousands of pieces," Mr. Kristiansen told Politiken. "Everything was so well preserved that you could hardly see it had been laying there for nearly 75 years."

(New York Times, 08/03/2017)

You can now complete the table:

Title:	
Any subtitles? ☐ Yes ☐ No	How Many:
Any paragraphs? ☐ Yes ☐ No	How Many:
Fiction or non-fiction?	
How much of the text did you understand? Tick the correct one: ☐ All of it ☐ Most of it ☐ Some of it ☐ None of it	
Anything unusual about the text?	
Any new words that you came across?	
Anything else	

EXERCISE 2

4-3-2-1

Now you are going to read over the text again and apply the 4-3-2-1 tool to help you extract more information from the text. This tool helps you focus on what the main points are and check to see if there is anything you didn't understand.

4 Facts relating to the main topic?

1

2

3

4

3 Important things that I found out

1

2

3

2 Interesting things

1

2

1 question I still have

1

Learning Point 3

Another way to actively engage with a text that you are reading is to keep some simple questions in the back of your mind as you are reading through the text. This next strategy is called 5Ws +1H. This stands for:

What – is happening?   **Who** – is the main person/ people in the text?

Where – is it happening?   **Why** – did it happen?

When – is it happening?   **How** – did it happen?

EXERCISE 3

5 Ws + 1 H

Let's go back to the text on the Danish father and his son and see if you are able to answer those simple questions. Read over the text once more but this time keep the five questions in your mind and when you think you have come across an answer underline it in the piece. When finished reading then try and answer the following questions.

a.   What is happening? _____

b.   Where did it happen? _____

c.   When did it happen? _____

d.   Who is the main person/people? _____

e.   Why did it happen? _____

f.   How did it happen? _____

PAUSE AND REFLECT

1. What have you learned in this lesson?

_____
_____

2. How did you learn this?

_____
_____

3. How can you use what you learned in your schoolwork/study?

_____
_____

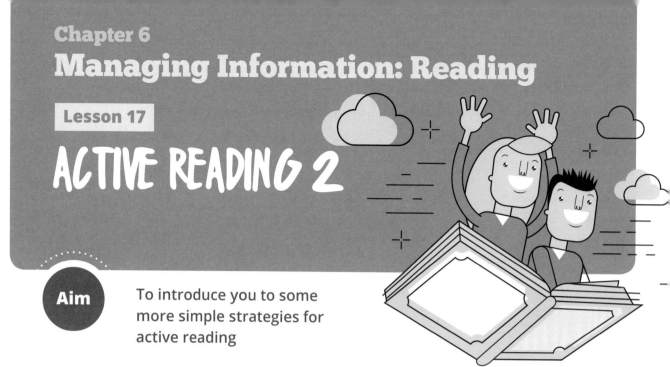

ACTIVE READING 2

Aim   To introduce you to some more simple strategies for active reading

 Learning Point 1

In the last lesson you looked at the difference between passive and active reading. In this lesson you will look at breaking a piece of text down to its subheadings and keywords.

A subheading is an additional heading that comes after the main heading in a text, breaking it up into smaller sections.

A keyword is an important word in a piece of text as it gives meaning to the text. These are the words that you need to remember.

This skill of being able to identify subheadings and keywords in texts will become very useful to you when you go to study. In Section 2 you will be introduced to POKER, which is a particular study based on extracting the subheadings and keywords for creating one-page summary notes of your texts.

 Subheadings and keywords

Below is an extract from a Business Studies chapter, read through the extract and complete the grid that follows.

Making the Most of Resources

What is a resource?

A resource is anything that we can use in order to meet our needs or achieve our goals. Resources include: materials, goods, people, knowledge, money and time.

Resources:

→   *Help us to achieve things*
→   *Are useful and valuable*
→   *Are often limited or scarce.*

Types of resources

Households and individuals have a variety of resources available to them, such as:

→ Physical/capital resources

→ Natural resources

→ Financial resources

→ Human resources

→ Time resources.

Physical/capital resources

These are goods that are made by people which can be used to provide other goods and services. These resources allow people to meet their day-to-day needs for food, clothing and shelter. They also provide us with the ability to travel, communicate and enjoy our leisure time.

Examples of physical or capital resources are:

→ Buildings and property

→ Vehicles

→ Computers

→ Equipment

→ Phones

→ Books

Natural resources

A household may have access to resources that are provided by nature, such as:

→ Land

→ Water

Financial resources

This category includes all types and sources of money available to households and individuals. These resources allow people to buy goods and services. Managing financial resources is a very important life skill which you will need to develop as you grow older. Studying business should help you develop that skill.

Examples of financial resources include:

→ Employment income

→ Income from benefits (e.g. child benefit)

→ Savings

→ Access to borrowing

Human resources

This refers to your skills, abilities and experience. It also includes all the other people available to help you. For example, if your school has a counsellor or a librarian, these are a valuable resource and you may be able to make use of their skills and expertise to assist you.

Examples of human resources are:

→ *An ability to read and write*
→ *An ability to solve problems*
→ *Skills in music, sport or technology, etc.*
→ *Creativity*
→ *Experience*
→ *Family and friends*
→ *Librarians*
→ *Teachers and coaches*
→ *Industry professionals*
→ *Community leaders.*

Time resources

Time is a valuable resource, so it is important to use it wisely. It is also our most limited resource and unlike many physical and financial resources, you cannot earn, borrow or buy more time.

However, if you make the best use of it, it will allow you to gather other resources, including education and skills that will help you achieve your goals. Time also allows you to work in order to earn the money needed to support your lifestyle.

(Time for Business, Junior Cycle Business Studies, Edco, Joe Stafford et al., 2016)

Headings

Subheadings

Keywords

Having read this extract, pick out the various subheadings and write these in first. Next go back through each subheading section and fill in the keywords associated with that subheading.

Chapter Title:

Subheading 1	Keywords		Sub heading 5	Keywords
Subheading 2	Keywords		Sub heading 6	Keywords
Subheading 3	Keywords		Sub heading 7	Keywords
Subheading 4	Keywords		Sub heading 8	Keywords

a. Do you feel you understand the topic better as a result of doing this? ☐ **Yes** ☐ **No**

b. Why?

_____

_____

EXERCISE 2

Exploring our keywords

Look at your list of keywords from Exercise 1 and decide in which column you want to write each word. If you have a word in column 1 or 2 then find the definition and fill it in in the space provided.

1. I don't know the word at all.	2. I've seen or heard the word but I don't know the meaning.	Definition if needed	3. I think I know the meaning.	4. I know the meaning.

PAUSE AND REFLECT

1. What have you learned in this lesson?

_____

_____

2. How did you learn this?

_____

_____

3. How can you use what you learned in your schoolwork/study?

_____

_____

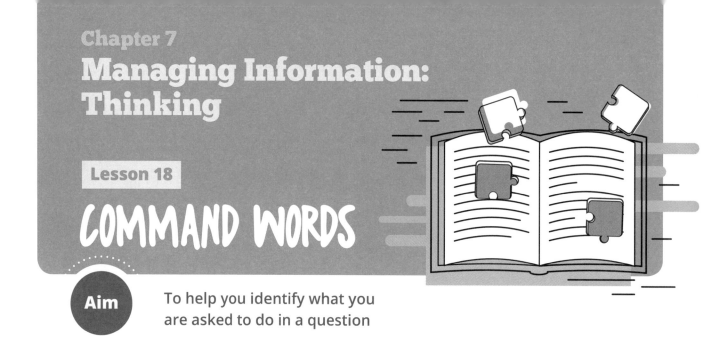

Chapter 7
Managing Information: Thinking

Lesson 18
COMMAND WORDS

Aim — To help you identify what you are asked to do in a question

 Learning Point 1

Having learned how you can engage more with any text you read, the next step is to look at how you apply what you have learned. In your class exercises, your homework and assessments you are asked to show what you have learned by being able to present it back to others when you answer questions.

This lesson looks at the most common types of questions asked and why they are asked. The command words in the question identify for you what you are supposed to do and what information is being required.

At the end of this lesson there are short explanations of the more complicated command words. You may wish to look at these as you do some of the exercises.

 EXERCISE 1

People in history

Read through the following piece of text on *A Farmer in Pre-Christian Ireland*, you will need to refer back to it throughout this lesson.

> **A farmer in Pre-Christian Ireland**
>
> *I am Fionn. Like most people in Celtic Ireland, my family and I make our living from farming. Life is not easy for us commoners. We do not own our own land, but rent it from a local warrior-nobleman.*
>
> *In return for our land, we must give him part of what we produce.*
>
> *Cows are our most important farm animals and they provide us with fresh milk all through the year. We also rear a few sheep and pigs. In autumn we*
>
> **PTO →**

sometimes slaughter an animal to provide us with salted meat for wintertime.

We grow wheat, barley and oats. Rotary querns are used to grind the grain, which is then used to make bread and porridge.

Farming is very important in Celtic society. Our goddess Brigid is the patron of spring and lambs. We honour Brigid at a festival called Imbolc, which is held on the first day of spring.

Another important religious occasion is Samhain (1 November), which is the Celtic New Year. The god Lug is honoured with animal sacrifices at the harvest festival of Lughnasa on 1 August.

Our priests, or druids, lead great ceremonies on religious festivals. Druids are learned men who have learned all about our customs and are believed to have magical powers. They along with filí (poets) and Brehons (judges) are all part of the Aos Dána, or nobility.

We live in a small house with walls of wattle and daub and a roof of thatch. Our dwelling is not as big or well protected as that of the local warrior. He lives in a dún on top of a nearby hill. A circular stone wall surrounds and protects the dún.

Although we are poor, we are not as badly off as the slaves who sometimes help us with the harvest. They were captured by our local warrior-nobleman and are now considered to be his property.

(New Complete History, Gill Education, Hayes, 2009)

EXERCISE 2

Knowledge

Now that you have read the text, you can begin to extract the relevant information from the text that is needed to build deeper understanding for learning. Knowledge is the fundamental basic information that you are required to remember in your exam. Extracting knowledge is the first step on the ladder of understanding and is based around the following questions/tasks:

> Who, what, why, where, when, which?
>
> Describe or define
>
> Can you find?
>
> Recall, select, list
>
> How did it happen?
>
> What were the main events?

Your task is to compile five questions based on *A Farmer in Pre-Christian Ireland* that if answered would show you have good knowledge of the text. **Try and answer your own questions.**

a. Question

Answer

b. Question

Answer

c. Question

Answer

d. Question

Answer

e. Question

Answer

EXERCISE 3

Comprehend

When you comprehend a text you have moved from simply absorbing the information contained to now beginning to manage and use that information. **The types of questions/tasks a student might come across here are:**

Describe in your own words
Summarise what you have learned
Classify, categorise the facts to show
What is the main idea of?
Compare and contrast
Can you explain what is happening?

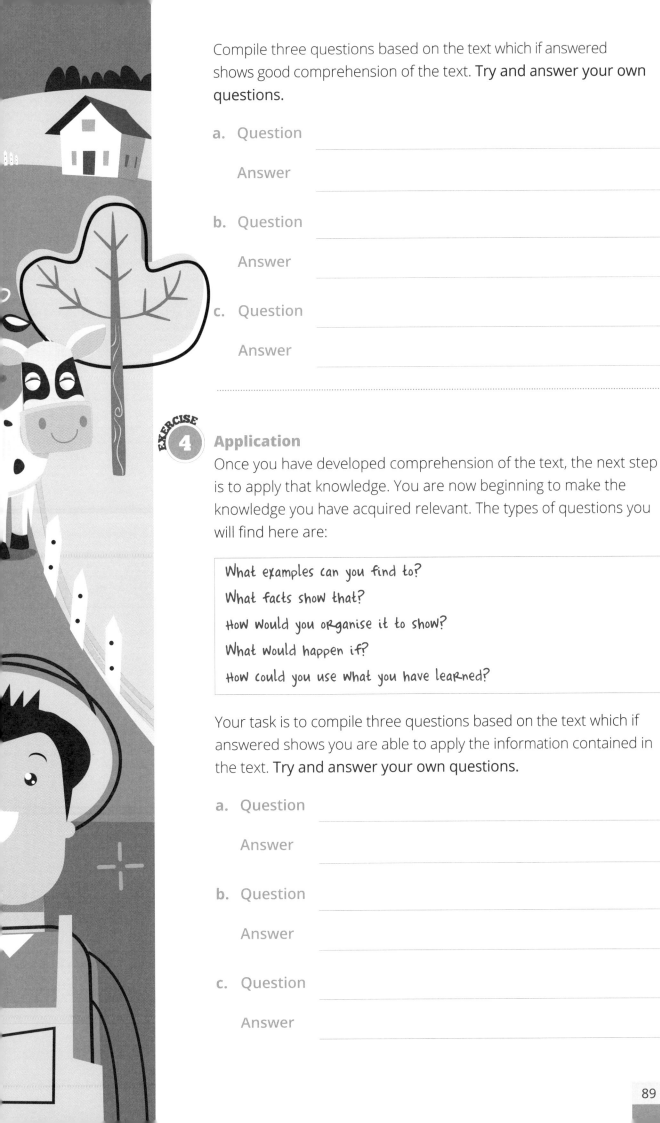

Compile three questions based on the text which if answered shows good comprehension of the text. **Try and answer your own questions.**

a. Question _____

Answer _____

b. Question _____

Answer _____

c. Question _____

Answer _____

EXERCISE 4 **Application**

Once you have developed comprehension of the text, the next step is to apply that knowledge. You are now beginning to make the knowledge you have acquired relevant. The types of questions you will find here are:

What examples can you find to?

What facts show that?

How would you organise it to show?

What would happen if?

How could you use what you have learned?

Your task is to compile three questions based on the text which if answered shows you are able to apply the information contained in the text. **Try and answer your own questions.**

a. Question _____

Answer _____

b. Question _____

Answer _____

c. Question _____

Answer _____

 **Learning Point 2**

Here are some explanations of the more complicated command words which may help you.

- **Classify / categorise:** Arrange people or things into groups according to shared or similar qualities.

- **Compare:** Identify the similarity between one thing and another.

- **Contrast:** Identify what is different between two opposing things or people.

- **Describe:** Give an account in words of (someone or something) including all of the relevant characteristics, qualities or events.

- **Explain:** Make an idea, situation or problem clear by describing it in detail, by giving the relevant facts.

- **Examine:** Inspect or investigate a piece of information in detail.

- **Summarise:** Condense the information given by identifying the relevant key points.

 PAUSE AND REFLECT

1. What have you learned in this lesson?

_____

_____

2. How did you learn this?

_____

_____

3. How can you use what you learned in your schoolwork/study?

_____

_____

 MENTAL NOTE

"The dictionary is the only place where success comes before work." – Mark Twain

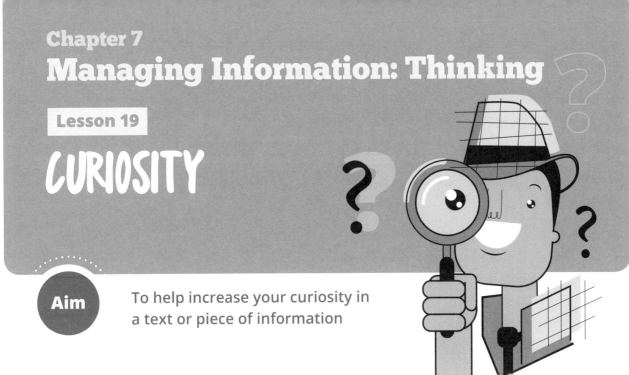

Chapter 7
Managing Information: Thinking

CURIOSITY

Aim To help increase your curiosity in a text or piece of information

Learning Point 1

If you are curious, then you become interested and so engage more easily in the learning. This lesson will give you some exercises that you can use to help you develop your curiosity and to think more deeply about a subject or topic.

EXERCISE 1

Problem Tree

A problem tree helps students to explore the causes, effects and possible solutions of an issue.

On the problem tree the roots represent the causes of the issue, the trunk is the issue itself, or problems, and the foliage represents the consequences or possible solutions.

Read the following passage and on your model of the tree identify what you think the problem is, what the possible causes are and finally what the possible consequences and solutions are.

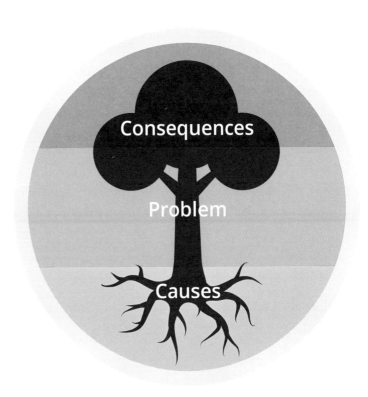

Consequences

Problem

Causes

Geography

Case Study: Irrigation in the Nile Valley, Egypt

The Nile is Africa's longest river. It rises in the highlands of east Africa and its total length is 6,671km. It flows northwards through the Sahara to the Mediterranean. Without the Nile, Egypt and its ancient civilisation would not exist.

Almost all the population of Egypt – 85 million – is found in less than 5 per cent of the country. People live in the floodplain of the river Nile and in the delta region.

Annual flooding

From ancient times, the Nile floodplain in Egypt was under water for several weeks every year because of rains in east Africa. When the water level fell, people grew crops on the damp soil. The soil was fertilised by sediments carried by the floodwaters. In the 1960s, construction of the dam began in Aswan to control flooding.

The Aswan High Dam

In 1975, the Aswan Dam was completed. The dam stores millions of tonnes of water in Lake Nasser. The dam means that water can now be released throughout the year through canals and plastic piping along farmland in the Nile valley. Therefore farmers can grow several crops in succession throughout the year. The farmland provides additional food for Egypt's growing population.

The disadvantages

There are disadvantages to the irrigation system in Egypt.

→ *The Nile floodplain no longer floods annually because waters are stored in Lake Nasser. Therefore, fertile sediments that covered the valley floor remain at the bottom of Lake Nasser. Now farmers have to buy expensive fertilisers.*

→ *The canals that distribute the irrigation waters in the valley are overrun with water snails, which carry an infection that affects humans.*

→ *Much water is lost because of evaporation from Lake Nasser.*

Future plans

Egypt is developing a major scheme to irrigate parts of the western desert. A canal will bring water from Lake Nasser to oases in the desert. Some people from the overcrowded Nile valley have migrated to these areas to begin a new life.

(Geoplant Geography for Junior Certificate, Educational Company of Ireland, Ashe & McCarthy, 2016)

a. Now fill in the blank template of the problem tree below using the text above.

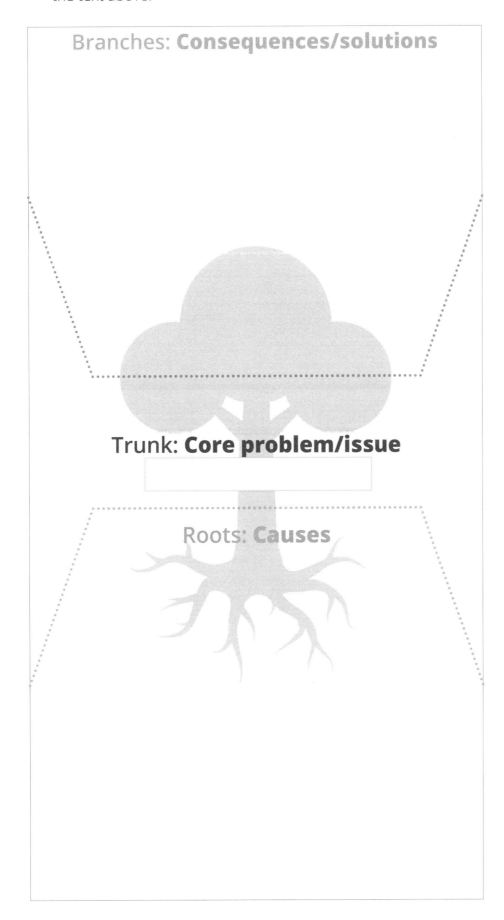

Branches: **Consequences/solutions**

Trunk: **Core problem/issue**

Roots: **Causes**

b. Now using this template again, choose another piece of text from another subject and complete.

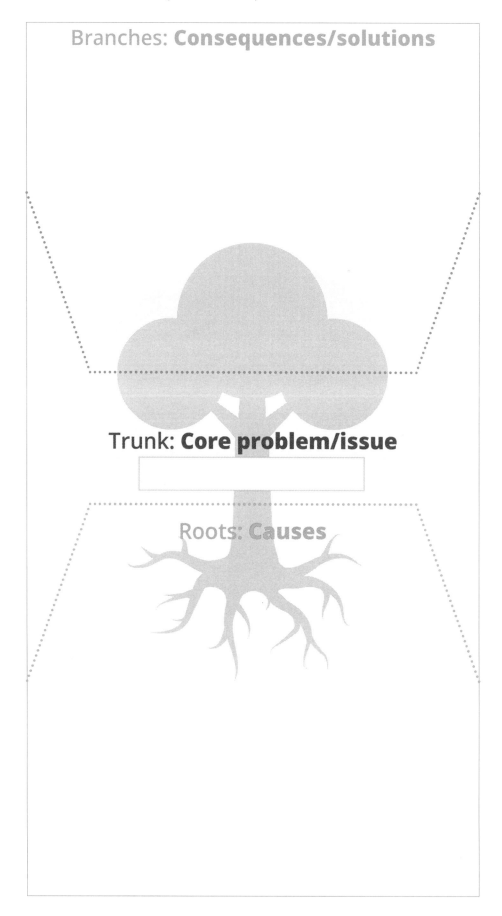

Branches: **Consequences/solutions**

Trunk: **Core problem/issue**

Roots: **Causes**

Avatar

This exercise will help you connect more with a topic by placing yourself remotely in the situation by creating your own avatar whom you can inhabit and go exploring with.

An avatar is a graphical image generated to represent you in a computer game or on an internet forum. Through your avatar, using your imagination you can experience and act in various situations.

For example, using the text above about desertification, imagine that your avatar is a member of the Tuareg tribe. Your avatar is meeting a journalist from the USA and wants to explain to them the following:

→   What desertification is

→   Its causes

→   How it is affecting your life

→   What can be done by you and others to help solve
      the situation.

In the box below write down what you think your avatar would tell the journalist.

Note: Other ideas for avatars

→ **History** – you create one avatar who is a time traveller and visits all the various key events in life.

→ **Modern Languages** – your avatar becomes a young person in their country trying to describe their life in various situations.

→ **Science and Maths** – your avatar could be a character from the Big Bang Theory or even a mad scientist carrying out wild experiments.

→ **Business Studies** – your avatar could be a young entrepreneur exploring all the facets of the business they have set up.

PAUSE AND REFLECT

1. What have you learned in this lesson?

2. How did you learn this?

3. How can you use what you learned in your schoolwork/study?

GRAPHIC ORGANISERS

Aim To show you some simple tools to help you organise your notes

Learning Point 1

Being organised in your learning not only means having a structure about when and how you learn but also being able to put some structure on the new information you are taking in. You do this by having notes. The most valuable notes that any student will ever own are the ones that they create for themselves.

A graphic organiser is a visual method of organising and summarising information that you need to learn. Graphic organisers are normally blank templates which you can download and fill in the information or you can create your own if you like.

This lesson will show you some simple graphic organiser templates which will help you make sense of large chunks of information that you may need to learn and recall at some point.

EXERCISE 1

Ranking Ladder

This organiser can be very useful to help you organise or prioritise information that you need to remember. Sometimes when we read text the actual sequence or order of events might not necessarily be evident. Here is a sample one from History to explain the feudal system, which shows the hierarchy or order of society in medieval times. This can also be very helpful when trying to remember the order of dates in history.

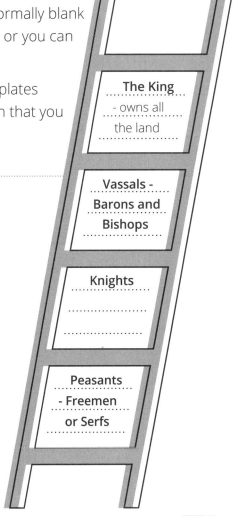

The King
- owns all the land

Vassals - Barons and Bishops

Knights

Peasants - Freemen or Serfs

Now create a ladder of your own for the following piece of text from Business Studies:

Making a complaint

If you discover a fault with a product you have purchased, you will need to make a complaint to the retailer. There are a few simple steps you should follow:

Step 1: *Stop using the item immediately.*

Step 2: *Bring the item back to the shop and ask to speak to the manager. If you still have the receipt or other proof of purchase, bring this with you. If the manager is unavailable, ask to speak to the person who has been left in charge in his/her absence.*

Step 3: *Explain the problem clearly, including details of purchase and when you noticed a problem with the item. Remain polite but firm. Know your rights under the Sale of Goods and Supply of Services Act 1980.*

Step 4: *Decide which form of redress you would prefer: a refund, a replacement or a repair.*

Step 5: *If the retailer does not offer a satisfactory result, you may need to send a written complaint providing details of the problem. Keep a copy of all correspondence.*

Step 6: *If the complaint is still not resolved, you may have to seek the advice of a third party, e.g. Competition and Consumer Protection Commission, Consumers' Association of Ireland.*

Step 7: *If the complaint is still not resolved, make a claim through the Small Claims Procedure, if applicable.*

Step 8: *Go to court.*

(Time for Business, Edco, Stafford et al., 2016)

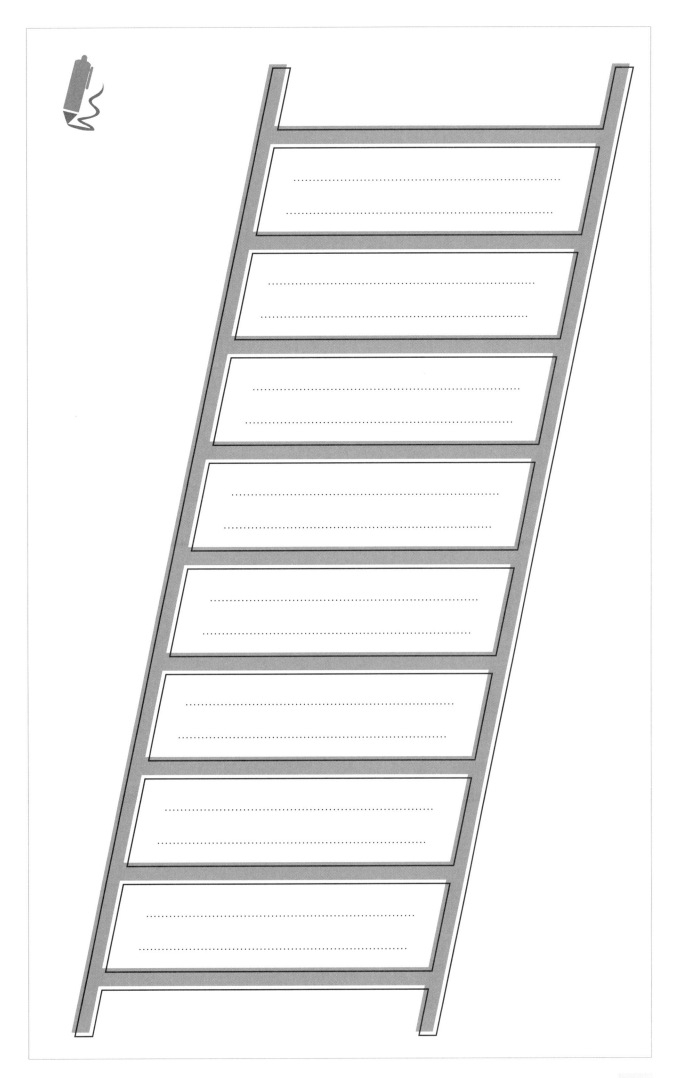

Learning Point 1

This graphic organiser is handy when trying to capture the link or connection between a series or sequence of information.

Here is an example from science for recalling the sequence of investigating changes in the state of water from solid to liquid to gas.

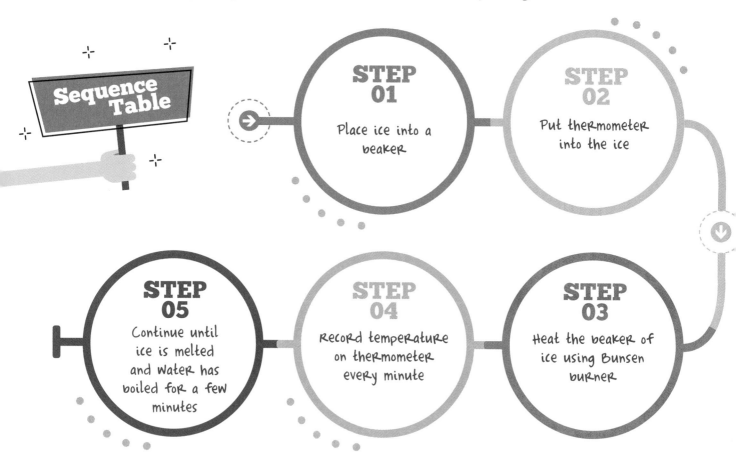

Sequence Table

STEP 01 — Place ice into a beaker

STEP 02 — Put thermometer into the ice

STEP 03 — Heat the beaker of ice using Bunsen burner

STEP 04 — Record temperature on thermometer every minute

STEP 05 — Continue until ice is melted and water has boiled for a few minutes

 EXERCISE 2 Try and create your own sequence for remembering how soil is formed.

How are soils formed?

A number of factors work together over a period of time to form soil. They are:

→ **Climate –** *Temperatures and rainfall influence the rate at which the parent rock is broken down by weathering. Hot climates experience chemical weathering, while colder climates experience freeze-thaw.*

→ **Parent material –** *The type of rock in an area also affects soil formation, for example, granite is slow to break down by weathering, while sandstone breaks down easily and forms soil quickly. Soils that develop from limestone are more fertile than those that develop from granite or sandstone.*

→ **Vegetation –** *When vegetation dies, it is broken down and decays to add humus and nutrients to the soil. Deciduous vegetation provides more leaf fall than coniferous vegetation.*

→ **Living organisms –** *Micro-organisms such as bacteria and fungi help to break down the dead plant and animal life in the soil, turning it into humus. As animals such as earthworms dig through the soil, they break it up and mix it, allowing more water and air to enter the soil. When these creatures die, their remains add nutrients to the soil.*

→ **Landscape –** *Upland areas are cold and wet, so soils are often waterlogged. There is little plant and animal life, so there is less humus. Lowland soils are generally deeper and well drained. They have more humus as there is plentiful plant and animal life.*

→ **Time –** *is one of the most important factors in soil formation. The longer a rock is exposed to the forces of weathering, the more it is broken down. It may take up to 400 years for 1cm of soil to form.*

(Geoplanet Geography for Junior Certificate, Edco, Ashe & McCarthy, 2016)

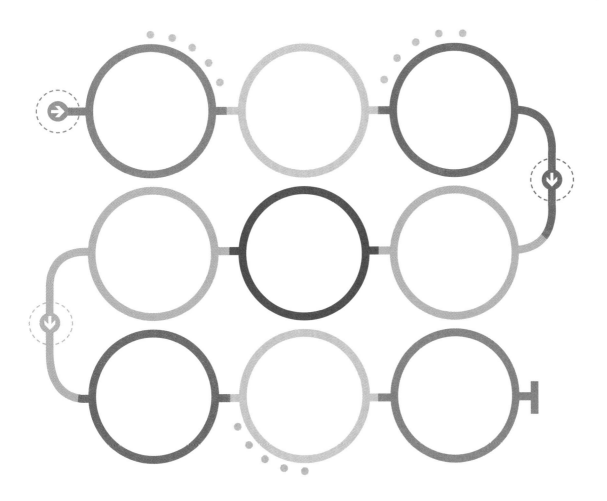

Choose any other subject and topic and see if you can create sequenced notes for the topic. Share with others in the class what you have done.

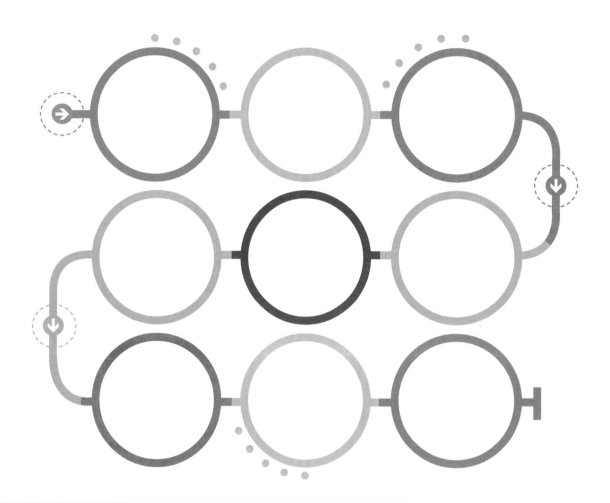

 PAUSE AND REFLECT

1. What have you learned in this lesson?

2. How did you learn this?

3. How can you use what you learned in your schoolwork/study?

Chapter 8
Managing Information: Note taking and writing

Lesson 21

WRITING FRAMES

Aim — To build your confidence in structuring your writing

 Learning Point 1

Having learned about common words that are used in questions the next step is to have some simple writing frames to help you structure your answers when answering questions.

A writing frame is simply a structure which you can use again and again when trying to write certain types of answers. This lesson looks at three different writing structures you need to answer questions. The three writing frames are:

(i) **Explanation**
(ii) **Instruction**
(iii) **Persuasion**

 Learning Point 2

Explanation. You use this frame when you are trying to discuss and explain why something happened. Here is an example of this using a piece of text and question from the history course.

Investigating the past

History is the story of our past. It is a wonderful story that tells us about things that happened, why they happened and why they were important.

Good historians are a bit like detectives. They search for evidence (clues) to find out about our past. Anything that provides such evidence is known as a source. There are two kinds of sources: primary sources and secondary sources.

(New Complete History, Gill Education, Hayes, 2016)

Question: explain why historians study the past?

Explanation writing frame

Subject: History	Topic: Investigating the past
Date: XX / XX / XX	

I want to explain why historians study the past.

The main reason is because history is the story of our past, telling us about things that happened, why they happened and why they are important to us.

Another reason is they search for evidence or clues to that past.

Explanation

Working with a learning partner:

- Choose a piece of text from either English, Geography or Business Studies

- Choose a question from the chapter on this text.

- Then answer the question using the explanation writing frame to help you.

Subject:	Topic:
Date:	

I want to explain why

The main reason is

Another reason is

Learning Point 3

Instruction. This writing frame is used when you would like to give information on how something should be done, the correct sequence that should be followed. Here is an example of this using a piece of text from your science course.

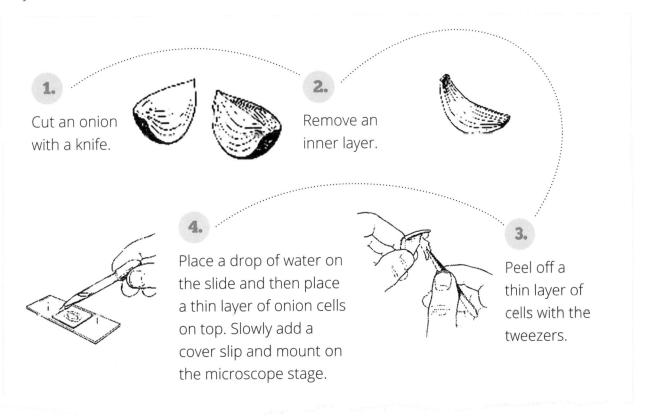

1. Cut an onion with a knife.

2. Remove an inner layer.

3. Peel off a thin layer of cells with the tweezers.

4. Place a drop of water on the slide and then place a thin layer of onion cells on top. Slowly add a cover slip and mount on the microscope stage.

Describe how you would prepare a specimen of onion cells for observation with a microscope.

Instruction writing frame

Subject: Science	Topic: Organisation of life

Date: XX / XX / XX

When we went to prepare a specimen of onion cells to view under a microscope

First we cut an onion with a knife and removed an inner layer.

Then we peeled off a thin layer of cells with tweezers.

Finally we placed the onion cells on top of a drop of water on the slide before adding the cover slip and placing on the stage of the microscope.

EXERCISE 2

Instruction

Working with a learning partner:

- Choose a piece of text which is giving instructions to follow from either Science, Technical Graphics or Home Economics.
- Choose a question from the chapter on this text.
- Then answer the question using the instruction writing frame to help you.

Subject:	Topic:
Date:	

When we

First we

Then we

Finally we

Learning Point 3

Persuasion. In this writing frame you are giving reasons for your opinion on a piece of text or trying to persuade someone else to agree with you. Here is an example of this using a piece of text from your English course.

Introducing a New Me - *Kallie Dakos*

There's a new ME this year,
An on-time ME,
A clean-desk ME,
A first to hand in assignments ME,
A teacher's-pet-for-the-first-time-in-my-life ME,
An-always-willing-to-be-good-and-help-out-ME,
A dead-serious-get-the-work-done-and-hand-it-in,
Before-it's-due ME.
The problem is
The new ME
Is not like ME
At all.
(Spirals New Junior Cycle English 1st Year, Edco, Campion et al., 2016)

Do you think this is a good poem for first years?

Persuasion writing frame

Subject: English	Topic: Poetry

I think that this is a good poem for first years.

Because it is talking about a new me at the beginning of the year.

Another reason I think this is because the student talking in the poem is trying to do everything right, just like everybody when they start school.

Furthermore the language is simple and it is easy for first years to understand.

Persuasion

Working with a learning partner:

- Choose a piece of text, either a poem or short story, from your English course.

- Choose a question that asks you to give your opinion on the text.

- Then answer the question using the instruction writing frame to help you.

Subject:	Topic:
I think that	
Because	
Another reason I think this is	
Furthermore	

PAUSE AND REFLECT

1. What have you learned in this lesson?

2. How did you learn this?

3. How can you use what you learned in your schoolwork/study?

MENTAL NOTE

"It's not a silly question if you can't answer it."
– Jostein Gaarder, Sophie's World

END OF SECTION REFLECTION

 Now that you have completed the first section of this programme, let's pause and reflect on all that you have learned.

In this part you will:

→ Reflect on the Junior Cycle key skills which you developed

→ Explore what you enjoyed most or least and why

→ Identify how you used what you learned in other areas of your studies

→ Identify possible areas you would like to focus on in the future.

Use the table below to rate your learning and performance from this section. Remember when considering your answers to reflect on all the variety of activities you engaged in during this section.

Managing Myself

1 Poor   **2** Fair   **3** Good   **4** Very Good   **5** Excellent

Key Skills		Student rating	Briefly Explain
Knowing myself			
I can ...	Recognise my personal strengths and weaknesses		
	Express my opinion		
Making considered decisions			
I can ...	Consider different options and ideas		
	Make plans and organise my work		
	Explain my choices to others		
Setting and achieving personal goals			
I can ...	Set personal goals		
	Ask for help when needed		
Being able to reflect on my learning			
I can ...	Evaluate and reflect on my learning		
	Receive and give feedback on my learning		
	Assess my own learning and suggest ways that I can improve		

Staying Well

1 Poor   **2** Fair   **3** Good   **4** Very Good   **5** Excellent

Key Skills		Student rating	Briefly Explain
Being confident			
I can ...	Communicate my opinions and beliefs with confidence in a variety of ways		
	Contribute to decision making within the class and group		
Being positive about learning			
I can ...	Find enjoyment and fun in learning		
	Learn from my mistakes and move on		
	Stick with things and work them through until I succeed		
	Recognise and celebrate my achievement		

Communicating

1 Poor   **2** Fair   **3** Good   **4** Very Good   **5** Excellent

Key Skills	Student rating	Briefly Explain
Listening and expressing myself		
I can ... Listen actively		
Express what I think and feel clearly in an appropriate tone		
Agree and disagree respectfully		
Ask well-thought-out questions and listen to the answer		
Use different styles of communication		
Performing and presenting		
I can ... Express my ideas through presentation such as design and graphics		
Make choices about how I can best present my ideas to others		
Discussing and debating		
I can ... Participate confidently in class discussion		
Present my point of view and be able to explain and support it		
Respond to opposite arguments constructively		
Using numbers and data		
I can ... Present, interpret and compare information using charts/diagrams.		

Key Skills		Student rating	Briefly Explain
Using language			
I can ...	Understand and use a wide vocabulary		
	Edit, correct and improve my written work		
	Use a range of forms to express my ideas.		

Being Creative

1 Poor   **2** Fair   **3** Good   **4** Very Good   **5** Excellent

Key Skills		Student rating	Briefly Explain
Imagining			
I can ...	Use different ways of learning to help develop my imagination		
Exploring options and alternatives			
I can ...	Think through a problem step-by-step		
	Try different approaches when working on a task		
	Seek out different viewpoints and consider them carefully		
	Repeat the whole exercise if necessary		
Implementing ideas and taking action			
I can ...	See things through to completion		
	Evaluate different ideas		
Learning creatively			
I can ...	Participate in learning in creative ways		
	Suggest creative ways that help me to learn		

Working with Others

1 Poor   **2** Fair   **3** Good   **4** Very Good   **5** Excellent

Key Skills		Student rating	Briefly Explain
Developing good relationships and dealing with conflict			
I can ...	Share my ideas honestly		
	Show respect for different points of view		
	Give and receive praise and criticism constructively		
Co-operating			
I can ...	Show appreciation for the contribution of other group members		
	Contribute to decisions as part of a group		
Learning with others			
I can ...	Work in pairs and larger groups to help each other when we are learning		
	Help other students to understand and solve problems		
	Recognise that others can support my learning and know how to get their support		

Managing Information and Thinking

1 Poor   **2** Fair   **3** Good   **4** Very Good   **5** Excellent

Key Skills		Student rating	Briefly Explain
I can ...	Look for new and different ways of answering questions and solving problems		
	Ask questions to probe more deeply		

Gathering, recording, organising and evaluating information and data			
I can ...	Recognise what I already know		
	Prepare and organise information and data so it makes sense to me and others		

Thinking creatively and critically			
I can ...	Question ideas and assumptions		
	Make connections between what I already know and new information		
	Adjust my thinking in light of new information		

Reflecting on and evaluating my learning			
I can ...	Reflect on and review my own progress		
	Identify barriers to my learning and suggest ways of overcoming them		
	Use a range of tools to help manage my learning		
	Keep believing that with continued effort I can succeed.		

1. Name three things you learned in this section?

   a. _____

   b. _____

   c. _____

2. What three things did you enjoy the most in this section?

   a. _____

   b. _____

   c. _____

   Why did you enjoy these?

   _____

   _____

3. Outline the three things which you found most difficult or challenging.

   a. _____

   b. _____

   c. _____

4. Name three things you have taken from this section and have begun to use in your other subjects.

   a. _____

   b. _____

   c. _____

NOTES

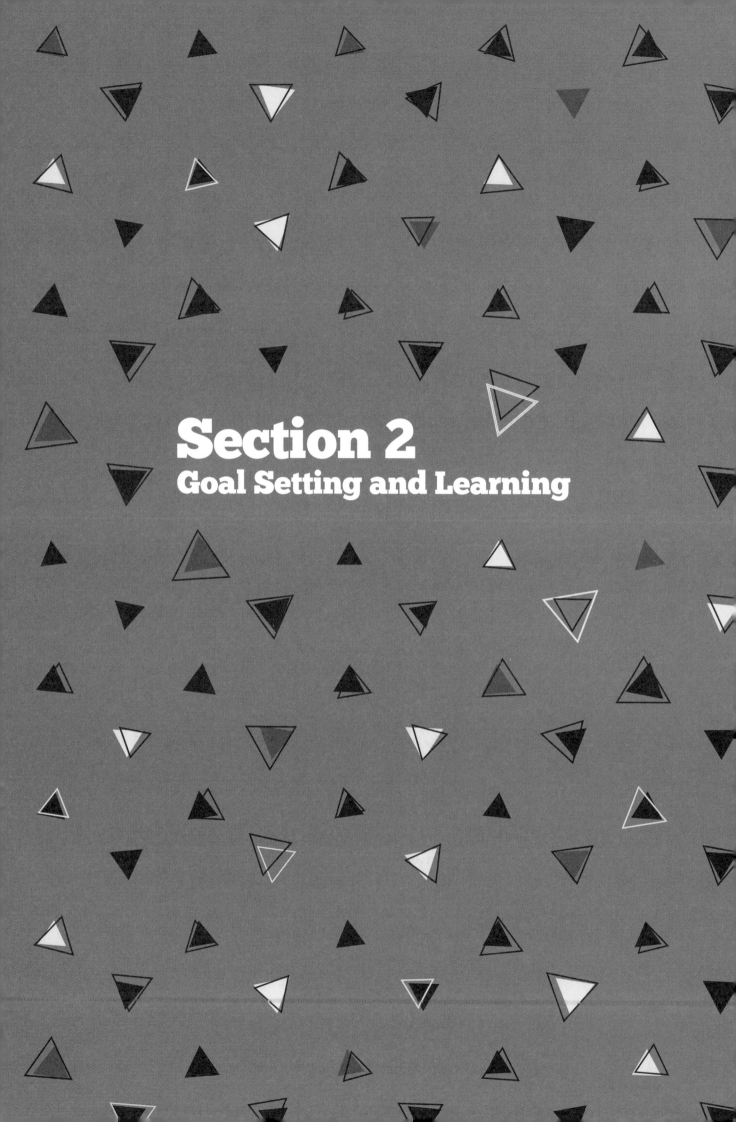

Section 2
Goal Setting and Learning

Introduction

During the first section you learned about how you learn and the skills for learning along with exploring various strategies which help you in your learning. This new section builds on what you have already covered by looking more closely at you as a learner, how to set goals for your Junior Cycle and finally provides you with a simple study system that will support you throughout the Junior Cycle and beyond.

Section 2 is broken into three component areas:

1. **You as a learner.** Here you build on the skills and behaviours for learning by developing your own intelligence profile which identifies your strengths as a learner.

2. **Goals and motivation for learning.** These lessons look at how you can use your learning strengths to set and achieve your own goals for learning by using the SUPER system. You explore your motivations for achieving your learning goals.

3. **Memory and Study.** The final section is where you learn about how memory works and here you are provided with some simple strategies to aid your memory. As study is key to helping you memorise what you need to recall for your assessments, you also look at what is involved in study. You learn all about planning your study, doing your study and reviewing what you have studied. As part of this section you learn about and practise POKER, an effective and proven study system.

Section 2
Goal Setting and Learning

Chapter 9
You as a Learner

Chapter 10
Setting my Goals

Chapter 11
Motivation

Chapter 12
Memory

Chapter 13
Plan it!

Chapter 14
Do it!

Chapter 15
POKER Practice

Chapter 16
Review It!

End of Section Reflection

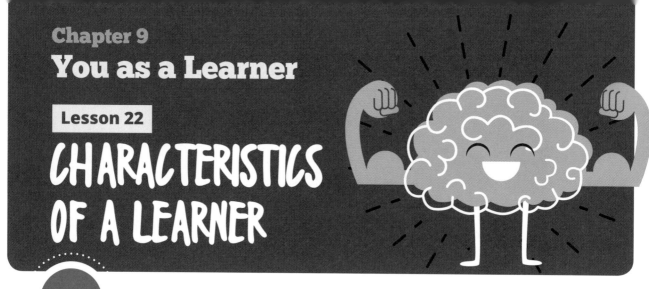

Chapter 9
You as a Learner

Lesson 22
CHARACTERISTICS OF A LEARNER

Aim — To help you identify qualities of an effective learner

 Learning Point 1

In the last section you explored both the rules for learning in class and the behaviours for learning. Do you remember what they are? Hopefully you have begun to implement them in your learning. This section begins by looking at how you have been doing on your journey to becoming a more effective learner by reviewing how well you have done on implementing these behaviours so far in your learning.

EXERCISE 1 — **8 Skills and Behaviours of an Effective Learner**

In this exercise you will rate yourself on how well you have been doing in practising the skills and behaviours as shown on the next page.

Read each statement and score yourself in relation to whether you feel this reflects you or not. The key is as follows.

1	**2**	**3**	**4**	**5**
I feel this is **almost never** true for me.	I feel this is **not often** true for me.	I feel this is **sometimes** true for me.	I feel this is **usually** true for me.	I feel this is **always** true for me.

Organised:
I have the right books and equipment for each class.

Hardworking:
I stick at an exercise even when I find it difficult.

Punctual:
I am on time for each class and hand up my homework on time.

Persistent:
I do my best in my work.

Co-operative:
I work well with other students in my class.

Thoughtful:
I think of others and their feelings.

Attentive:
I pay attention to what the teachers say.

Optimistic:
I try to find the best in every situation.

Where you score between **1 and 3** you are less likely to have developed this quality. Where you score **4 to 5** these are your strengths and they will assist you in becoming a good student and an effective learner.

EXERCISE 2

Reflecting on Your Score

Here are a few simple questions which will help you think about your answers in the previous exercise and possibly think about how you could improve your score for some of the behaviours.

a. What skills and behaviours did you score highest on?

_____

b. Can you give examples of when you did these things?

_____

_____

c. Did you score low on any behaviour?   ☐ **Yes** ☐ **No**

d. If yes, which ones?

_____

_____

e. What could you do to improve your scores?

_____

_____

f. Do you think learning about these skills and behaviours will help make you a more effective learner? ☐ **Yes** ☐ **No**

g. Give a reason for your answer.

_____

_____

h. Did any of the skills and behaviours of a good learner surprise you by being on the list? ☐ **Yes** ☐ **No**

Explain: _____

_____

_____

PAUSE AND REFLECT

1. What have you learned in this lesson?

_____

_____

2. How did you learn this?

_____

_____

3. How can you use what you learned in your schoolwork/study?

_____

_____

MENTAL NOTE

"The knowledge of all things is possible."
– Leonardo da Vinci

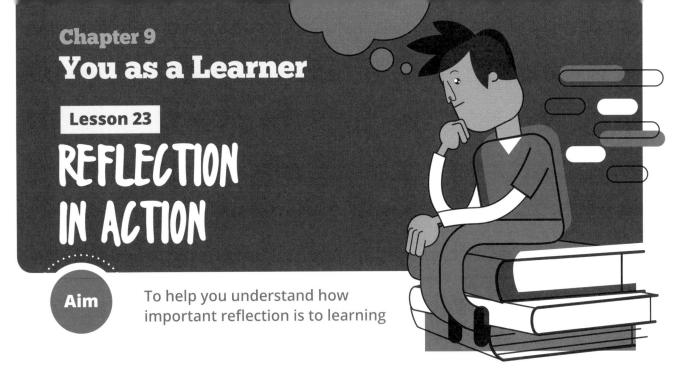

Chapter 9
You as a Learner

Lesson 23
REFLECTION IN ACTION

Aim To help you understand how important reflection is to learning

 Learning Point 1

A key element of learning is the ability to reflect on what and how you learn and being able to apply that learning in the future. Reflection is the way you extract the personal learning from an experience so that you can use what you have learned again at some point in the future.

 Why Reflect?

Below is a list of the benefits of reflection. Read through each one and give an example of where you were able to demonstrate this benefit in the past in your learning.

Here is an example of one for you. Can you now give examples for the others?

Example

In the last lesson I identified that I had learned the skill of being organised.

Now I use my homework journal better to help me be more

organised.

a. I really enjoy doing group work.

b. I find it difficult working on my own on written exercises.

_____

_____

c. I try to work with a learning partner on written exercises.

_____

_____

d. When we do group work I get to discuss my ideas with others.

_____

_____

e. I am able to make connections between different things that I learn.

_____

_____

f. I am able to see how I can use what I learned.

_____

 Learning Point 2

You now know what the benefits of reflecting on your learning are but do you know what good reflection is? Whilst you may write reflections on many things, there are common features of a good reflection, known as **IDHR**. These are:

I = You relate it back to what you learned i.e. I learned.

Detail = You write a clear account of what you learned, giving as much detail as possible.

How = You explain how you learned something.

Relate = How will you use what you have learned again in the future?

 Features of a Good Reflection

Here are two examples of student reflections on a project they completed for CSPE. Read through each one and decide whether you think this reflection is either **Above Expectation** or **Below Expectation**.

Give as much detail in your reason for your grading as possible. Remember, even if it is **Below Expectation** there are still some positive aspects to the reflection, be sure to include these in your answer.

Title of Project: OUR World

Date of Project: XX/XX/XX

How much did you enjoy this project?

Why? It was great fun working with other people in my class.

What did you do? The class made a film about our lives and the world we live in.

The most important thing you learned was? Teamwork

Why? We struggled at times to agree with each other.

What challenged you the most? Having to agree with others.

How could you overcome this challenge in the future? Agree with others.

What new skills did you learn? I learned new IT skills in filmmaking.

How could you overcome this challenge in the future? I'm not sure.

Above Expectation / **Below Expectation**

Reasons for answer:

Example two:

Title of Project: OUR WORLD
Date of Project: XX/XX/XX

How much did you enjoy this project?

Why?

I really enjoyed this project because I got to learn exciting new skills involved in filmmaking. I had never made a film before and didn't know what was involved. We had great fun trying to decide what we were going to make the film about.

What did you do?

I did a filmmaking project where a group of us from the class made a 4-minute film giving an insight into our lives as teenagers and our outlook on the world around us. We had to decide on what we would make the film about, how we were going to make the film and who was doing what job. We showed the film to our whole school at assembly one morning.

The most important thing you learned was?

Learning how to work together as a team to achieve something.

Why?

I learned so much about what was involved in teamwork, like conflict resolution for when we didn't all agree about things, and the various roles and responsibilities people have when working in a team.

What challenged you the most?

Working as part of a group, we didn't always agree on things and had to figure out how to do it together.

How could you overcome this challenge in the future?

I developed skills like listening to others and compromising, which I will use in future.

What new skills did you learn?	Along with the teamwork skills, I also developed new IT skills in filmmaking. These skills included filming and using IT software like PowerPoint and Movie Maker.
How could you overcome this challenge in the future?	I will be able to use my teamwork skills in other classes when we are asked to do group work and also when I'm with my friends. I can use my IT skills for other projects in other subjects, like using PowerPoint to make presentations in class.

 **Above Expectation** / **Below Expectation**

Reasons for answer:

 PAUSE AND REFLECT

1. What have you learned in this lesson?

   _____

   _____

2. How did you learn this?

   _____

   _____

3. How can you use what you learned in your schoolwork/study?

   _____

   _____

Lesson 24
INTELLIGENCE PROFILES 1

Aim — To help you identify your strengths when it comes to learning

 Learning Point 1

Why do you think you do better at one subject than another or you prefer one subject over another? You probably think you only have one intelligence, when in fact you probably have at least 8 and you probably use only 3 to 4 of them continually. Professor Howard Gardner referred to these as your **Multiple Intelligences**. The question is not about how intelligent you are but rather where your intelligences are or simply where your talents lie. Talents are those things that come more easily to you. This explains why you find some subjects easier than others or enjoy some subjects more than others.

WHERE DO YOUR TALENTS LIE?

SKILLS

Multiple Intelligences

Here is a diagram with your 8 intelligences; take some time and read through them. Write down any of the intelligences that you might not understand. You can ask your teacher to help explain these to you.

What intelligences did you not understand?

_____

_____

_____

_____

EXERCISE 2

Characteristics of the Intelligences

Below is a list of the various intelligences followed by a description of characteristics of each one. Match the correct description with the correct intelligence from the list. Read through each description and fill in its number beside the correct intelligence.

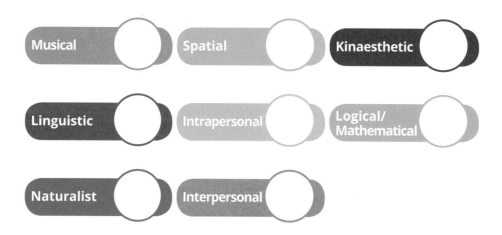

Musical ◯   Spatial ◯   Kinaesthetic ◯

Linguistic ◯   Intrapersonal ◯   Logical/ Mathematical ◯

Naturalist ◯   Interpersonal ◯

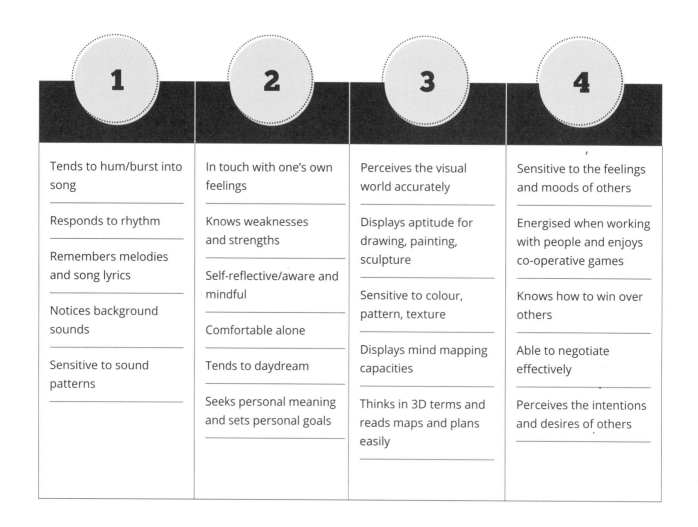

1	2	3	4
Tends to hum/burst into song	In touch with one's own feelings	Perceives the visual world accurately	Sensitive to the feelings and moods of others
Responds to rhythm	Knows weaknesses and strengths	Displays aptitude for drawing, painting, sculpture	Energised when working with people and enjoys co-operative games
Remembers melodies and song lyrics	Self-reflective/aware and mindful	Sensitive to colour, pattern, texture	Knows how to win over others
Notices background sounds	Comfortable alone	Displays mind mapping capacities	Able to negotiate effectively
Sensitive to sound patterns	Tends to daydream	Thinks in 3D terms and reads maps and plans easily	Perceives the intentions and desires of others
	Seeks personal meaning and sets personal goals		

5	6	7	8
Sensitive to the natural world	Enjoys language	Needs to be active, plays sports or enjoys activities	Sees connections
Ability to recognise pattern or species in the natural and built environment	Likes word games, good at spelling	Likes to make or build things	Analyses/categorises
Capacity to see things in relationship to one another	Has a feel for sentence structure	Uses hands when talking	Spots flaws in arguments
Ability to classify and categorise types and models of species	A good story teller	Well co-ordinated	Enjoys numbers
	Enjoys puns and riddles	Uses tactile sense to communicate	Abstract thinker
	Likes the sound and rhythm of words		Systematic approach
	Enjoys reading		

PAUSE AND REFLECT

1. What have you learned in this lesson?

   _____

   _____

2. How did you learn this?

   _____

   _____

3. How can you use what you learned in your schoolwork/study?

   _____

   _____

Chapter 9
You as a Learner

INTELLIGENCE PROFILES 2

Aim — To help you identify your strengths when it comes to learning

 Learning Point 1

The next five exercises will help you identify which intelligence you use most and help you create your own intelligence profile. There are many advantages to building your own profile, one of which is identifying your strengths. By knowing where your strengths lie you can build on these. Nobody is good at everything but it's important to know what you are good at and use this to your advantage. Sometimes you might not realise that you are good at lots of things.

By working to your strengths you become a more confident learner, building on past successes and possibly willing to take on new challenges which you might not have had the confidence to do in the past.

EXERCISE 1 **Identify Your Intelligence 1**

Tick the intelligences which you believe you use the most, you can choose between 2 and 5.

This is an intuitive response. If you enjoy singing you might tick musical, good at languages you might tick linguistics, enjoy being around people you might tick interpersonal. Most people have 2-5 areas that they are relatively comfortable with.

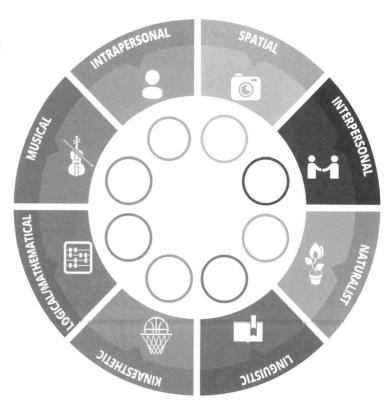

Identify Your Intelligence 2

NOW LET'S TAKE ANOTHER LOOK ...

Here are some descriptions of the various attributes associated with each intelligence.
Place a tick beside the ones that you think best describe you.

Musical

- ○ Enjoy sound in nature
- ○ Interested in music
- ○ Enjoy hearing and/or making music
- ○ Good sense of rhythm and/or melody
- ○ Easily learn and retain music.

Total ticks: ○

Intrapersonal

- ○ Like to daydream and imagine
- ○ Enjoy doing things independently of others
- ○ Appreciate privacy and quiet for working and thinking
- ○ Understand your own feelings and thoughts and why you do things
- ○ Think about the relevance of what you are doing and learning.

Total ticks: ○

Spatial

- ○ Good sense of direction
- ○ Observant, see things others do not notice
- ○ See things clearly in your mind's eye, e.g., a familiar room
- ○ Films, slides, videos help learning
- ○ Use charts, diagrams, maps easily.

Total ticks: ○

Interpersonal

- ○ Can help with difficulties between people
- ○ Sensitive to others' moods and reactions
- ○ Interested in how others think and feel
- ○ Involved in clubs or other types of group activity
- ○ Enjoy teamwork, discussing and co-operating with others.

Total ticks: ○

Naturalist

- ○ Gets angry about pollution and destruction of nature
- ○ Appreciates scenic places
- ○ Feels alive when in nature
- ○ Conscious of changes in the weather
- ○ Notices nature above other things
- ○ Yearns to be outside as much as possible
- ○ Is sensitive to birds, animals and plants.

Total ticks: ○

Linguistic

- ○ Like books, plays, poetry, radio, conversations. Enjoy language
- ○ Learn well from books, tapes, lectures, listening to others
- ○ Fluent, expressive talker with a well-developed vocabulary
- ○ Good at explaining things
- ○ Like to write things down.

Total ticks: ○

Kinaesthetic

- ○ Like to deal with problems physically, get directly involved, get 'hands on'
- ○ Skillful when working with things
- ○ Enjoy sports, games, physical exercise
- ○ Like to be moving, doing or touching something you are learning about
- ○ Remember best what you have done (as compared to seen/ heard).

Total ticks: ○

Logical/Mathematical

- ○ Like to solve puzzles and problems
- ○ Like logical explanations
- ○ Arrange tasks in a sensible, orderly sequence
- ○ Look for patterns and relationships between things
- ○ Approach tasks in a logical, step-by-step manner.

Total ticks: ○

EXERCISE 3

Identify Your Intelligence 3

LET'S TAKE A CLOSER LOOK ... Below is an activity list associated with each intelligence. Place a tick in the box of each activity that you see yourself good at, or that you imagine you could be good at if you tried.

Musical	Intrapersonal	Spatial	Interpersonal
○ Writing music	○ Planning your own time	○ Drawing diagrams	○ Good friend
○ Playing an instrument	○ Understanding your feelings and moods	○ Understanding plans of a house	○ Listening carefully
○ Repeating lyrics of songs with ease	○ Working on your own	○ DIY furniture assembly	○ Managing/Supervising others
○ Moving in time to music	○ Keeping a diary/journal	○ Art/Drawing	○ Member of a club
○ Good sense of rhythm	○ Recognising who you're like/unlike in your personality	○ Visualising images in 3-D	○ Teaching/Training others
○ Clapping or beating time with music	○ Achieving personal goals	○ Reading maps for a journey	○ Parenting
○ Remembering slogans, raps, verses	○ Striving for constant improvement	○ Driving, parking	○ Committee work
○ Selecting appropriate music for an event	○ Self-motivation	○ Crafts	○ Leadership skills
○ Humming while working	○ Finding time to be on your own	○ Jigsaws	○ Helping others with personal problems
○ Selecting background music	○ Predicting what you will be able to do well or have difficulty with before you begin		○ Any group work
Total ticks: ○	**Total ticks:** ○	**Total ticks:** ○	**Total ticks:** ○

Naturalist	Linguistic	Kinaesthetic	Logical/Mathematical
○ Enjoys gardening and working with plants	○ Giving verbal instructions	○ Sports	○ Mathematics
○ Enjoys being outdoors	○ Giving written instructions	○ Dancing/Physical movement with good coordination	○ Science
○ Likes to hike, walk or climb	○ Filling in forms	○ Car maintenance	○ Making lists
○ Keeps pets	○ Writing letters	○ DIY jobs	○ Accounts
○ Recognises different types of birds, animals and plants	○ Explaining something clearly	○ Cooking, baking	○ Budgeting
○ Campaigns on environmental issues	○ Crosswords, word search puzzles	○ Hand-held puzzles (Rubik's Cube, etc.)	○ Planning time
○ Watches natural science programmes	○ Verbal arguments	○ Juggling	○ Calculating scores in games/sports
	○ Creative writing or writing in general	○ Keeping children actively occupied	○ Working out timetables
	○ Reading literature	○ Anything active	○ Managing money
	○ Reading or writing poetry	○ Hobbies that require specific hands-on skills (model building, knitting or others)	○ Calculating scores on bets
Total ticks: ○	**Total ticks:** ○	**Total ticks:** ○	**Total ticks:** ○

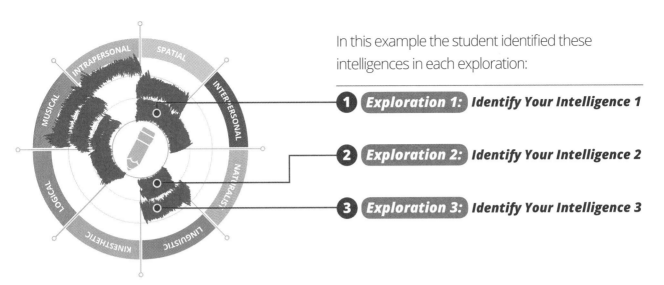

In this example the student identified these intelligences in each exploration:

1 **Exploration 1:** *Identify Your Intelligence 1*

2 **Exploration 2:** *Identify Your Intelligence 2*

3 **Exploration 3:** *Identify Your Intelligence 3*

EXERCISE 4

Now Complete Your Own Profile

On the chart below you can fill in your results for each exercise.

Step 1: On the innermost circle shade in what you said were your top intelligences, up to five.
(Identify your Intelligence 1).

Step 2: Now go back to **Identify your Intelligence 2**. Count up the ticks you had in each column and shade in the next circle your three top scoring intelligences.

Step 3: Go to **Identify your Intelligence 3**. Do the exact same thing, add up your ticks in each column. Then shade in the outer circle your three top scoring intelligences. See example on next page.

Now create your own.

 **Learning Point 2**

Here is what your results mean:

1. The intelligences where you shaded in all three circles are your strongest intelligences. These are the ones you use all the time naturally and serve you the best, the ones you are most comfortable with.

2. The intelligences shaded in two circles are still strengths for you but they are not as natural. As a result you can and will do them with ease when asked but you will have to be asked.

3. The intelligence where you have only one circle shaded, you can use now and again, when the need arises. They are called the *'I will if I have to'* intelligences! They are there for you but you may not see them as your greatest strengths.

4. And finally ... the intelligences you left completely blank, these are your *'No way, not me! Ask someone else'* intelligences. You may feel like you are not strong in that area or maybe it is something you feel you have not been able to grasp. Either way it is an intelligence that you actually have but you are not, for whatever reason, using it enough to benefit you.

....

 So What Does This Tell Me?

Having completed this exercise you may wish to reflect on what you have learned about yourself. Ask yourself the following:

a. What were your top three intelligences?

(i) _____

(ii) _____

(iii) _____

b. (i) Are the answers what you expected?　　☐ **Yes** ☐ **No**

Explain: _____

_____

_____

_____

c. It is good to build on your strengths and know your main intelligences, so what does this tell you about what type of learner you are?

_____

_____

_____

Learning Point 3

You now know what your strongest intelligences are, these are the ones you use naturally all the time and are your strengths when it comes to learning. In the next lesson you will explore all about working to your strengths and how working to your strengths further helps you in becoming a more effective learner.

PAUSE AND REFLECT

1. What have you learned in this lesson?

_____

_____

2. How did you learn this?

_____

_____

3. How can you use what you learned in your schoolwork/study?

_____

_____

MENTAL NOTE

" It's not how smart you are, it's how you are smart." – Howard Gardner

Lesson 26

WORKING TO MY STRENGTHS

Aim To learn to work to your strengths

 Learning Point 1

Your multiple intelligences profile will have highlighted some of your strengths when it comes to learning. Working to your strengths is an empowering experience. The image below illustrates how working to your strengths builds your confidence as a learner. When you do well, sometimes you receive praise. Praise is a positive affirmation. Such affirmations make you feel good about what you have just achieved. When you feel good about your achievements you are more likely to work harder when faced with a challenge in the future as your confidence has increased.

Strength **Affirmation** **Positive Feeling** **Confidence**

Here is an example:

One of Anne's intelligences was linguistics. This meant that one of Anne's strengths was studying languages. She found that she did very well at school in French and always got good results and praise from her teachers in her assessments. When Anne was on holidays in France with her parents she began to use what French she had because she felt confident about her ability from all the affirmation she received. At the end of the holiday Anne realised that her French had really improved.

Your Strengths

Let's begin by looking at the example of Anne.

a. What was Anne's strength and why was this one of her strengths?

_____

_____

b. Why do you think Anne used her French when she was away on holidays?

_____

c. Why do you think Anne's French improved?

_____

_____

Now, about you

d. From your list of multiple intelligences what are your top three strengths?

   (i) _____

   (ii) _____

   (iii) _____

e. Give an example of how you might have developed each of your top three strengths in the past.

   (i) _____

   (ii) _____

   (iii) _____

f. How do you think you could develop these top three strengths further in the future?

   (i) _____

   (ii) _____

   (iii) _____

⚙ Learning Point 2 Gift to You

Being part of a strong group can be very encouraging and supportive. Everybody has different strengths which they can bring to the group. You have already looked at the various elements of being part of a group.

Here is a chance for you to encourage the strengths of everybody in your class group as well as gain some positive affirmations for yourself. Remember, **affirmations** are positive statements which help you feel better about yourself and encourage you to keep going. Share your book around so others can write one strength that they can identify in you.

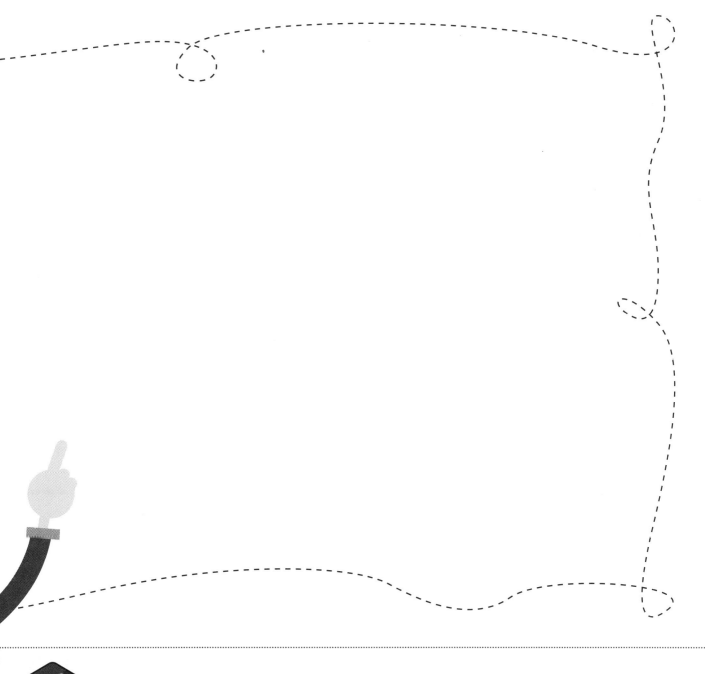

 PAUSE AND REFLECT

1. What have you learned in this lesson?

_____

_____

2. How did you learn this?

_____

_____

3. How can you use what you learned in your schoolwork/study?

_____

_____

Chapter 10
Setting my Goals

Lesson 27
CREATING GOALS TO SUCCEED

Aim   To help you create your own goals for success

EXERCISE 1

Letter to Me

This lesson will begin by you doing a little bit of dreaming. What you have to do is to think about where you are now in life and what you would like to achieve for yourself in the next two years.

Now write yourself a short letter from the future and imagine that you have already achieved all you set for yourself to achieve in the next two years. In your letter don't write about the things you will do but rather write about what you will achieve and how you will feel once you have achieved it. Try and create an image of what it feels like to have succeeded.

Dear Me,   Future Date:_____

_____

_____

_____

_____

_____

_____

_____

Yours,

Learning Point 1

So let's turn your dream into reality. An important step to achieving this is by setting yourself goals for the future. A goal is a specific outcome which you want and commit yourself to achieving. An example could be 'I want to do well in my English by achieving an above expectation result.'

People who succeed at anything have a clear vision of or a goal of what it is they want to achieve. Before you set yourself any 'big' goals it is handy to do a quick check of what you have available to you that can help you on your way. In the previous lesson you have already identified what your strengths as a learner are so now is a good time to begin to think how you can use these strengths to be successful in your learning.

A **SOAR** analysis is a simple tool which you can use as a quick checklist of where you are and what resources you have at hand to help you achieve your goal.

SOAR stands for **Strengths, Opportunities, Aspirations, Resources**

You already have a good idea now of what your learning strengths are but this diagram will help explain what the other words mean.

Here are some questions that can help you complete a SOAR analysis.

Strengths

→ What are you good at, your strengths and skills? *E.g. sports, IT, mixing with others*

→ What do your family and friends think you are good at?

→ What special knowledge or skills do you have?

Opportunities

→ What opportunities are out there for you? *E.g. support from family, friends, school, clubs*

→ What could help you build your skills and strengths?

→ How can you use the skills and strengths you have? *E.g. helping others in school.*

Aspirations

→ What are you passionate about? *E.g. playing hockey, reading, films, music*

→ What do you want to do and achieve? *E.g. do well in Junior Cycle, win championship trophy*

→ What would it look like if you already achieved it? *E.g. received high grades in Junior Cycle, won championship trophy.*

Resources

→ What resources/assistance do you need to help you meet your aspirations? *E.g. support from teachers/coach, extra training.*

EXERCISE 2 — My SOAR

Now here is your opportunity to do your own SOAR analysis. Try to fill in the SOAR template with as much information as you can.

Learning Point 2

After completing your SOAR analysis you hopefully now have a greater awareness of your strengths and resources and what aspirations and opportunities you have for the future. In the next lesson you will be able to use this information to help you create some learning goals.

PAUSE AND REFLECT

1. What have you learned in this lesson?

_____

_____

2. How did you learn this?

_____

_____

3. How can you use what you learned in your schoolwork/study?

_____

_____

Chapter 10
Setting my Goals

Lesson 28
THE SUPER SYSTEM 1

Aim To learn how to achieve your goals

 Learning Point 1

Now that you have completed your SOAR analysis the next step is to begin to put your goal into action. To do this you can follow the SUPER system. This success system gives you a simple strategy or way to achieve any goal you set yourself.

S SEE
See the success.

U UNDERSTAND
Understand how you can make it happen.

R REWARD
Reward yourself after you achieve your goal.

E EXECUTE
Execute and take action every day.

P PLAN
Plan how you can make it happen.

Exercise 1 — See Your Success

The next few exercises will bring you through the SUPER system so you will know how it works and be able to use it again and again in the future.

Let's go back to your dream but this time you are going to describe it as a goal. What you need to do is to decide on what your goal is and write it down. **Be specific**, give as much detail as possible.

Here is an example of two types of goals. Place a tick beside the goal you think is the best and then explain why you think so.

a. My goal is to increase my grades in English by summer in second year. ⬭

b. My goal is to improve in English. ⬭

Explain your choice:

_____

Exercise 2 — Your Goal

Now write the top three goals you want to set yourself for the Junior Cycle.

Goal 1: _____

_____

Goal 2: _____

_____

Goal 3: _____

_____

Learning Point 2

The next step in the SUPER system is understanding why your goal is important to you. This is your motivation for achieving your goal. Motivation is the why behind your goal. Why are you going to make the effort to achieve it, why is it so important to you that you achieve it? If you are not motivated enough then you will just give up on your goal and it ends up being simply a dream again.

EXERCISE
3

Understand It

For each goal, outline why it is important to you – what is your motivation?

Goal 1: _____

_____

Goal 2: _____

_____

Goal 3: _____

_____

PAUSE AND REFLECT

1. What have you learned in this lesson?

_____

_____

2. How did you learn this?

_____

_____

3. How can you use what you learned in your schoolwork/study?

_____

_____

Aim To learn how to achieve your goals

 Learning Point 1

In the last lesson you had looked at setting yourself some goals for the Junior Cycle and begun to explore the SUPER system which can help you achieve your goals. Do you remember what SUPER stands for?
You have already looked at See it and Understand it, so this lesson will explore the rest of the SUPER system.

 Learning Point 2

Let's begin with Plan it. Before you begin any project or task or even go on a journey you need to plan exactly what you need to do. This involves breaking your goal into the various actions or steps needed to achieve your goal. This becomes your plan of action.

For example, you want to improve your grades in English by summer of second year, so what do you do?

Step 1: You decide how much extra time you are going to spend studying English each week.

Step 2: You create a new study plan to reflect this.

Step 3: You look at your English course and break it down into its various topics.

Step 4: You begin to take each topic and study it.

Step 5: You give yourself regular tests to see how you are progressing.

EXERCISE 1

Plan it

Now go back to your goals that you wrote down in the previous lesson and complete the action steps needed to achieve your goals.

Goal 1:

Step 1 _____

Step 2 _____

Step 3 _____

Step 4 _____

Step 5 _____

Goal 2:

Step 1 _____

Step 2 _____

Step 3 _____

Step 4 _____

Step 5 _____

Goal 3

Step 1 _____

Step 2 _____

Step 3 _____

Step 4 _____

Step 5 _____

 **Learning Point 3**

Now the next step is to put that plan into action. Don't forget, a goal remains a dream unless you take action. Action is the key to success, you can have all the goals and plans you like but unless you put them into action nothing happens.

Here is the simple formula that any successful person will tell you is the key to success.

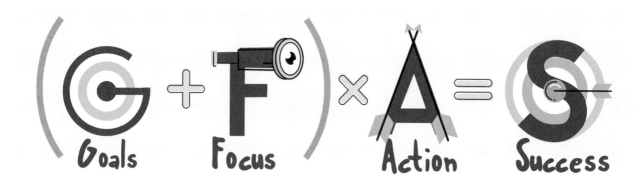

Goals + Focus × Action = Success

As you can see from this simple formula, action is the multiplier, how successful you are depends on the amount of effort or action you put in.

So **zero action = zero success   high action = high success**

 Action

Review your goals by looking at your first goal, ask yourself the following questions:

a. Do you really feel you are going to put
   in the effort?   ☐ **Yes** ☐ **No**

b. What will this effort involve?

   _____

   _____

c. What supports do you need in achieving your goal?

   _____

   _____

 **Learning Point 4**

Once you have achieved your goal you should reward yourself, to acknowledge and recognise your effort and commitment.

 EXERCISE 3

Reward

For each of your goals think about how you might possibly reward yourself when you have achieved them.

Goal 1 - Reward: _____

Goal 2 - Reward: _____

Goal 3 - Reward: _____

 EXERCISE 4

Quick Recap

Can you remember without looking back what each of the letters means in the SUPER system? See if you can write them down. Remember, don't look back unless you really need to.

S = _____

U = _____

P = _____

E = _____

R = _____

You learned about affirmations previously? Rewards are like affirmations. They can boost your confidence and encourage you to take on other challenges and set yourself other goals, possibly even something you might not have considered before. Especially now that you have the SUPER system to aid you.

 PAUSE AND REFLECT

1. What have you learned in this lesson?

   _____

   _____

2. How did you learn this?

   _____

   _____

3. How can you use what you learned in your schoolwork/study?

   _____

   _____

Lesson 30

EXPLORING MOTIVATION

Aim — To help you explore the concepts of motivation and resilience

 Learning Point 1

In the last two lessons you looked at setting yourself goals and how using the SUPER system can help you achieve these goals. Do you remember the formula for success?

$$(Goals + Focus) \times Action = Success$$

You will undoubtedly meet obstacles along the way to achieving your goal which can throw you off course for a while. It is at these times that you need to stay motivated and develop a skill called **resilience**.

Resilience is the ability to start again or bounce back when you meet an obstacle. You will learn more about it in Section 3.

 Learning Point 2

As you know, motivation is the why behind you doing or achieving something.

There are two main types of motivation:

a. **Extrinsic motivations** are those that exist outside of yourself such as rewards, trophies, praise from others, money.

b. **Intrinsic motivations** are those that arise inside yourself such as personal gratification, feeling better about yourself, boosting your own confidence.

Your Motivations

Go back to your goals and look at what you wrote down for 'Understanding' each goal. Now for each why or reason you wrote can you decide whether the motivation is extrinsic or intrinsic? You may even have both for the one goal. For each, write the motivation/s and after each one state whether it is extrinsic or intrinsic.

Goal 1 - Motivation: _____

_____

Goal 2 - Motivation: _____

_____

Goal 3 - Motivation: _____

_____

How Motivated Are You?

Use the star rating to rate how motivated you are in the following areas:

★ ☆ ☆ ☆ **Not Motivated At All**

★ ★ ☆ ☆ **Fairly Motivated**

★ ★ ★ ☆ **Motivated**

★ ★ ★ ★ **Extremely Motivated**

Event	Rate your motivation
Do well in my school	☆ ☆ ☆ ☆
Get a job	☆ ☆ ☆ ☆
Go to college	☆ ☆ ☆ ☆
Be a healthy person	☆ ☆ ☆ ☆
Do well at a hobby	☆ ☆ ☆ ☆
Be a good person	☆ ☆ ☆ ☆
Complete all homework	☆ ☆ ☆ ☆
Remember all materials for school	☆ ☆ ☆ ☆
Be a good friend	☆ ☆ ☆ ☆
Be on time	☆ ☆ ☆ ☆
Try to listen	☆ ☆ ☆ ☆

Learning Point 3

From the previous exercise you might realise that sometimes you are not necessarily as motivated as you could be. Here are five simple tips that might help you increase your motivation.

1. **What's in it for me?**

   Ask yourself how you can benefit from putting in the extra effort.

2. **Introduce a challenge**

   If you find something too easy then you can get bored very easily and give up. Giving yourself small challenges can be a great motivator as you can feel a sense of accomplishment when you overcome the challenge. Be careful not to overdo it though, if something becomes too difficult it can equally become a de-motivator.

3. **Take control**

   You can feel more motivated when you feel like you have more control over what is going to happen. The key is to focus on what you can do in a situation, not what others can do.

4. **Focus on the journey,**

   not the outcome. Focus on achieving individual action steps as it gives you a sense of accomplishment along the way.

5. **Make it fun**

   No matter what age you are you can always have fun. If you can introduce an element of fun or enjoyment into what you are doing, it can increase your motivation greatly.

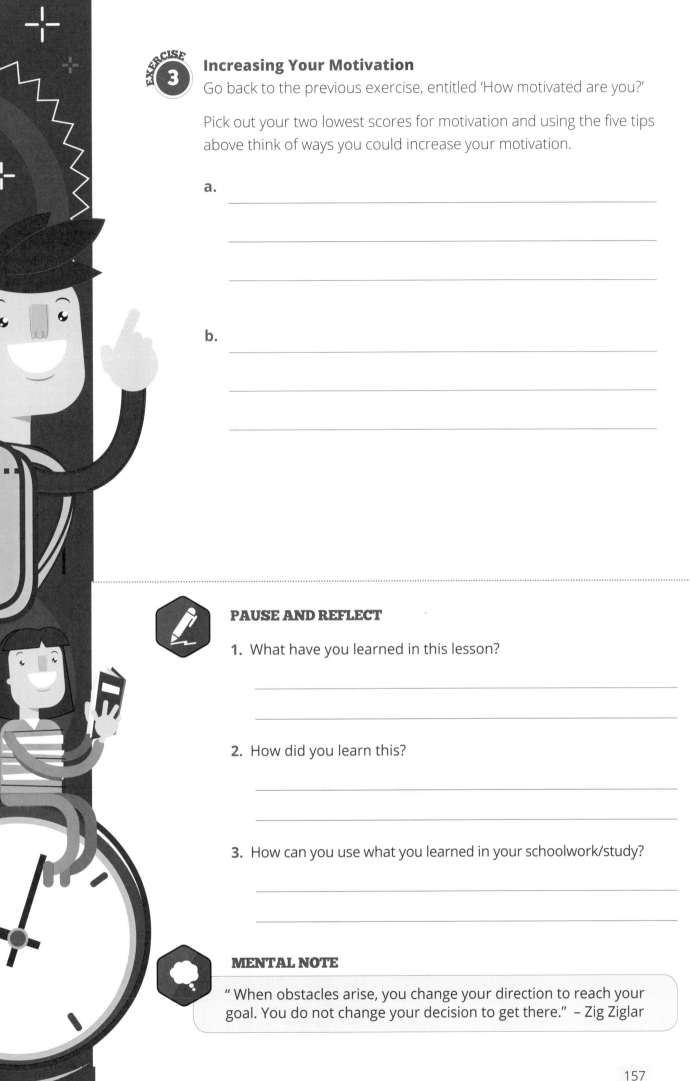

EXERCISE 3

Increasing Your Motivation

Go back to the previous exercise, entitled 'How motivated are you?'

Pick out your two lowest scores for motivation and using the five tips above think of ways you could increase your motivation.

a. _____

_____

_____

b. _____

_____

_____

PAUSE AND REFLECT

1. What have you learned in this lesson?

_____

_____

2. How did you learn this?

_____

_____

3. How can you use what you learned in your schoolwork/study?

_____

_____

MENTAL NOTE

" When obstacles arise, you change your direction to reach your goal. You do not change your decision to get there." – Zig Ziglar

Chapter 11
Motivation

Lesson 31
BELIEVING IN YOURSELF

Aim — To begin to develop a sense of self-belief

 Learning Point 1

Self-confidence is an important contributor to achieving goals. You have read about how positive affirmations and rewards help boost your confidence. Confidence is all about believing in yourself. This lesson explores what confidence or self-belief might look like and how others can help build your self-confidence.

 EXERCISE 1

What Does Confidence Look and Sound Like?

a. Here are some images of young people who might be displaying signs of low self-confidence. Can you match the correct explanation to the correct image?

1. Unconfident body language
2. Not joining in on activities
3. Being shy or timid
4. Succumbing to peer influence

b. Now here are some images of young people who are displaying signs of self-confidence. Can you match the correct explanation to the correct image?

1 Good posture

2 Alert eyes

3 An ease at giving and receiving praise

4 A relaxed walk

5 A curiosity about new ideas

6 A refusal to give up when things turn out differently than planned

 **Learning Point 2**

Did you know that self-belief relies on others too? You can take in the messages others give you and turn those messages into beliefs, particularly negative ones! To help you work on self-belief you need to surround yourself with people who will build you up with positive messages. These will boost your confidence and self-belief.

Some people create an imaginary 'Believer Network' for themselves. The network's job is to provide wisdom, advice and affirmation to you.

The believers should be people you respect, admire and trust. Your believers should also know you. The point of this exercise is to make your own 'Believer Network'. By having people who believe in you, you become a believer in yourself.

 Believer Network

Name five people you have in your believer network and give a reason why you are choosing each person.

1

Name: _____

Reason: _____

2

Name: _____

Reason: _____

3

Name: _____

Reason: _____

4

Name: _____

Reason: _____

5

Name: _____

Reason: _____

EXERCISE 3 — The Beliefs

Now that you have chosen your believer network, what type of advice or positive messages do you think they would give you? Imagine what they would say to you and write some of the messages in the speech bubbles below.

Positive comments from my believer network.

PAUSE AND REFLECT

1. What have you learned in this lesson?

   _____

   _____

2. How did you learn this?

   _____

   _____

3. How can you use what you learned in your schoolwork/study?

   _____

   _____

Chapter 11
Motivation

Lesson 32
CHANGING BELIEFS

Aim — To challenge your belief systems

 **Learning Point 1**

There is something self-fulfilling in the way people speak to themselves internally – teachers, students, everybody. Beliefs can become so engrained that they define everything you do and everything you don't do! Beliefs are the thoughts you have about whether something is true or not. The diagram shows the TEAR model, which explains how the beliefs or thoughts we have can affect the outcome.

"If you think you can or you think you can't, you are right."
Henry Ford

→ **Cycle of Beliefs TEAR – Thoughts, Emotions, Actions and Results**

- Thoughts define feelings
- Emotions determine actions
- Actions govern results
- Results reinforce thinking

So your actions are determined by your emotions and your emotions by your thoughts. So if you want to change the results of your actions then you must first change your thoughts and beliefs. An example would be if you believe that you are no good at languages, then you won't want to put in the effort and, guess what, you will find that you are not getting the grades you could be.

EXERCISE 1

What Do I Believe About Myself?

It is really important that you challenge some of the negative messages you might receive by reminding yourself about all of your good and positive attributes. Try and fill in as many balloons as possible with positive beliefs about yourself.

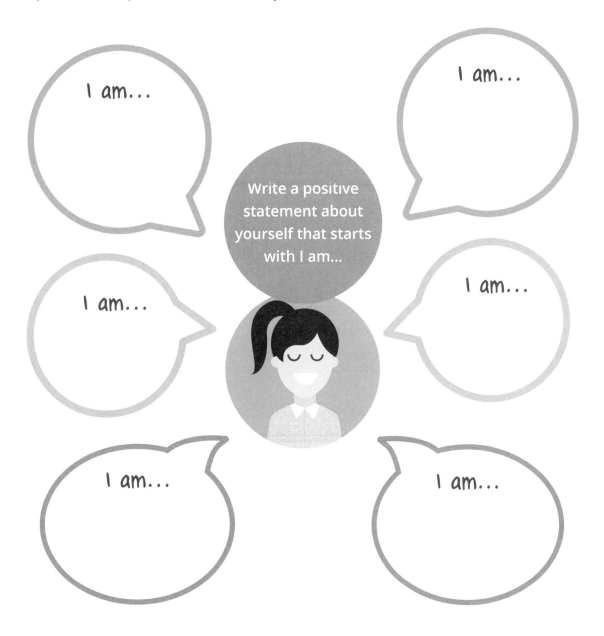

EXERCISE 2 — Negatives and Positives

In the following exercise think of one negative belief you might have about yourself then try and turn that negative belief into a positive.

For example:

I'm shy

When I get to know people I am a good friend.

Learning Point 2

Your mind is made up of two parts: the **subconscious** and the **conscious**.

The **subconscious mind** is like an app running in the background, all the time. It holds all the unseen information that you use without even thinking, all you have ever thought, seen, or done in your whole life. Without you knowing, it is working out how you feel, what you remember and what you believe.

You are thinking, planning, and making decisions all the time with the **conscious mind**. This is the part you are aware of. However, the conscious mind only does what the subconscious mind agrees with. If the subconscious mind doesn't agree with a thought, fact, feeling or opinion from the conscious mind, then the conscious mind will reject it without question.

Your **belief system** is the filter between your conscious and subconscious mind. The thing about your beliefs is not whether or not they are true but the fact that your subconscious believes them to be true, because if your subconscious believes it to be so then the conscious will make it so.

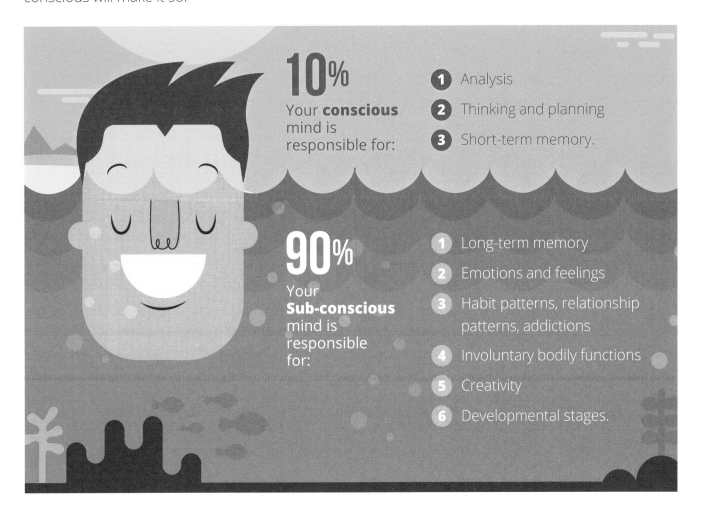

10%

Your **conscious** mind is responsible for:

1. Analysis
2. Thinking and planning
3. Short-term memory.

90%

Your **Sub-conscious** mind is responsible for:

1. Long-term memory
2. Emotions and feelings
3. Habit patterns, relationship patterns, addictions
4. Involuntary bodily functions
5. Creativity
6. Developmental stages.

However, you might not often be aware that your feelings and other parts of your subconscious impact everything you do consciously. For example: *You plan a trip to the zoo. This is a conscious decision. You pack the picnic, buy tickets, work out bus times etc. Subconsciously you are excited, you desire to go to the zoo, you have fond memories of the zoo from when you were younger. However, if you have had a negative experience before you would not even plan a trip to the zoo because you believe you would not enjoy it.*

Your beliefs therefore are linked strongly to your subconscious. You may not even KNOW consciously that you feel a certain way about something, you just DO. The next exercises will help you explore how beliefs impact behaviour.

EXERCISE 3 Read the following story about Jen and then answer the questions that follow.

Jen's Beliefs

Case Study:

Jen is 14 years old. She adores playing soccer and has played since she was 5 years old. Jen lives with her grandparents. They are not very interested in her soccer playing as they believe succeeding in school is much more important for her to succeed in life.

Her grandparents never completed secondary school, they believe it is the most important thing she can do. Jen believes the only way she will ever be happy is by playing soccer and earning lots of money from doing so!

She is a good student, but she doesn't believe she should try any harder than she already does. She is happy to just pass her assessments once she is staying out of trouble and playing soccer.

a. What are Jen's beliefs?

_____

b. What are her grandparents' beliefs?

_____

c. What beliefs might be limiting Jen?

_____

d. What beliefs might be helping Jen?

_____

e. Should Jen change any of her beliefs? Why?

_____

f. Should her grandparents change any of their beliefs? Why?

_____

g. How might Jen begin to start changing her beliefs?

_____

h. How does Jen feel?

_____

i. How do her grandparents feel?

_____

EXERCISE 4

Your Beliefs

Now let's explore some of your beliefs and how well they are serving you. Write in one belief under each heading, and answer the key questions on each belief.

Beliefs About School

Is this a helpful belief? ☐ Yes ☐ No	**Why?**
Should I change this belief? Why?	

Beliefs About Me

Is this a helpful belief? ☐ Yes ☐ No	**Why?**
Should I change this belief? Why?	

PAUSE AND REFLECT

1. What have you learned in this lesson?

   _____

   _____

2. How did you learn this?

   _____

   _____

3. How can you use what you learned in your schoolwork/study?

   _____

   _____

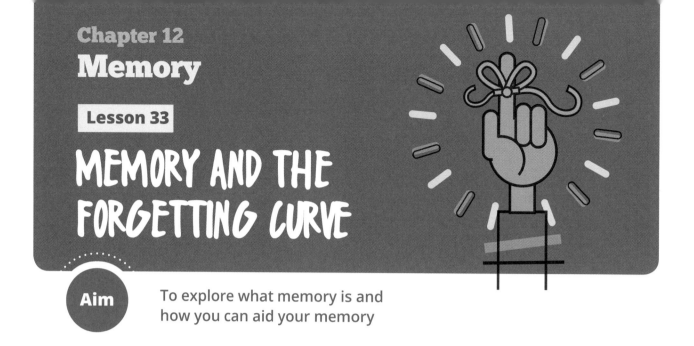

Chapter 12
Memory

Lesson 33

MEMORY AND THE FORGETTING CURVE

Aim To explore what memory is and how you can aid your memory

 Learning Point 1

During this course you have been looking at how the brain works and various functions of the brain. Here you will look at memory.

Memory is not the job of one little filing cabinet in your brain. Memory is a function of many areas of the brain. Riding a bike, for example, uses many parts of the brain.

Our memories have a great capacity for remembering, but if we do not REINFORCE learning, we will naturally forget! The Forgetting Curve shows how much we actually do forget, in the absence of regular review to reinforce memory. After just 24 hours you will have forgotten 80% of what you learned in a class, for example. After one week, you are down to forgetting 90%.

The Forgetting Curve

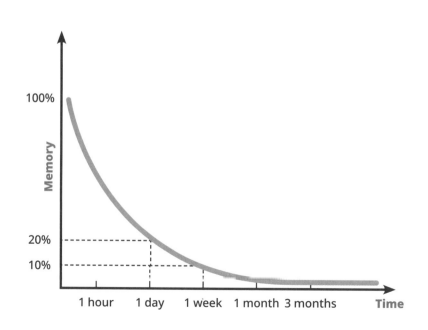

The memory of how to operate a bike comes from one area, the memory of how to get from here to there comes from another, the memory of cycling safety rules from another, and that nervous feeling when a car veers dangerously close comes from still another.

What Do I Remember?

a. Write down the names of three topics you have studied in Science this term:

_____

_____

_____

b. Write or draw quickly what you remember about any of these topics.

c. Did you do any homework on these topics at any time AFTER you were first introduced to them in class? ☐ **Yes** ☐ **No**

d. Are you surprised by the amount of material you can recall?
☐ **Yes** ☐ **No**

Explain: _____

_____

_____

_____

EXERCISE 2

My Memory is PERFECT!

Now try and answer the following questions:

a. What is your favourite movie?

_____

b. How many times have you seen it?

_____

c. What is it about?

_____

d. Write down any characters, lines or songs you remember from the movie.

_____

_____

e. What is your favourite song?

_____

f. How often do you listen to the song?

_____

g. Write down any lines from the song you remember.

_____

h. Do you remember the names of all the students in your class? ☐ **Yes** ☐ **No**

i. Write down their initials.

_____

j. How often do you hear the names of the people in your class?

_____

k. Finally, have you noticed why you have recalled all this information so easily? ☐ **Yes** ☐ **No**

l. Can you explain why you are able to recall all this information?

_____

 Learning Point 2

Hopefully you will have noticed it is much easier for you to recall information when it is more familiar or you keep receiving the information regularly. This is what is called ETCHing it in your mind. There are three simple ways to help you ETCH something in your memory, making it easier for you to recall. They are:

(i) **Repetition** – frequently repeating something over and over again.

(ii) **Association** – creating a link or association with what you are trying to recall with what you already know.

(iii) **Imagination** – This is where you use your imagination to again associate words with images in your mind.

For example:

People tend to think in images rather than words. When you hear banana you see a banana and not the letters b-a-n-a-n-a.

Over the next two lessons you will explore some simple memory techniques which will help you ETCH information into your memory. You will also come across etching again when you are introduced to your POKER study system.

 PAUSE AND REFLECT

1. What have you learned in this lesson?

_____

_____

2. How did you learn this?

_____

_____

3. How can you use what you learned in your schoolwork/study?

_____

_____

MEMORY TECHNIQUES 1

Aim To explore some simple memory aids

 Learning Point 1

While many people rely on repetition to learn and be able to recall information, there is an easier way – by simply using your imagination to associate words with images in your mind.

Remember, there are three keys to accessing your memory:

(i) Imagination

(ii) Association

(iii) Repetition

These next two lessons will introduce you to some simple mnemonics. Mnemonics is a word which describes a variety of activities or techniques that you can use to aid your memory. These simple techniques will help you in your learning and make it easier for you to recall information even when under pressure.

 Learning Point 2

Acronyms

This is one of the simpler ones. You create an acronym to remember a list of words. To do this:

1. Take the first letter from each of the words you want to recall.

2. Create a catchy new word with these letters.

3. The individual letters from the new catchy word help you recall the words you need to memorise.

A common example would be **FAT DAD**… the counties of Northern Ireland:

Fermanagh   **A**ntrim   **T**yrone   **D**erry   **A**rmagh   **D**own

EXERCISE 1

Create your own acronyms to help you recall the following:

a. **Gaeilge** – The adverbs that take a 'séimhiú' or 'h' are *Ar, do, foai, roimh, um, thar, sa*

_____

_____

b. **English** – Elements of a poem – *alliteration, image, mood, onomatopoeia, rhythm, simile, technique*

_____

_____

c. **Science** – Organisation of life – *organelle, cell, tissue, organ, system, organism, population, community, ecosystem*

_____

_____

> The word doesn't necessarily need to exist or make sense but you need to be able to pronounce it so you can recall it when you need to.

 Learning Point 2

Silly Sentences

Using humour and imagination can really help when trying to recall lists or facts. Silly sentences are a bit like acronyms but instead of creating a new word, each first letter is converted into a silly sentence.

Here is an example:

Mercury	**M**y
Venus	**V**ery
Earth	**E**legant
Mars	**M**om
Jupiter	**J**ust
Saturn	**S**erved
Uranus	**U**s
Neptune	**N**ine
Pluto	**P**ancakes

EXERCISE 2

Create your own silly sentences to help you memorise:

a. **History** – Elements of a medieval monastery – *Refectory, cell, guest house, oratory, cloister, scriptorium, chapter house*

_____

_____

b. **Business Studies** – Types of income – *Wages/salaries, pensions, child benefits, jobseeker's benefits, family income supplement, interest on savings, dividends on shares, windfall*

_____

_____

c. **Geography** – Factors influencing mass movement – *Gradient, water, vegetation, human activity*

_____

_____

PAUSE AND REFLECT

1. What have you learned in this lesson?

_____

_____

2. How did you learn this?

_____

_____

3. How can you use what you learned in your schoolwork/study?

_____

_____

MENTAL NOTE

" Self-education is, I firmly believe, the only kind of education there is." – Isaac Asimov

Chapter 12
Memory

Lesson 35

MEMORY TECHNIQUES 2

Aim   To explore some simple memory aids

 Learning Point 1

This lesson is a simple continuation of the previous lesson and will explore two more simple memory aids:

a. The Story Method

b. The Roman Room Method

 Learning Point 2

The Story Method

We all love stories and remember what happens in a good story. You can use this to help you remember facts, by putting them into a story. What you do is make up a story with words that remind you of what you are learning. It is important that you do not repeat any of the words though.

Here is an example for you:

We met a lovely girl called SHANNON. Shannon picks up her wheelBARROW. She walks to the edge of the SHORE (SUIR). She looks out at the BLACKWATER. She tries to row out to sea but she is told by the lifeguard that there is a BAN (BANN) on rowing as the boat has NO OARS (NORE).

Do you know what the words you were trying to remember are?

Answer: They are the longest rivers of Ireland, the Shannon, the Barrow, the Suir, the Blackwater, the Bann and the Nore.

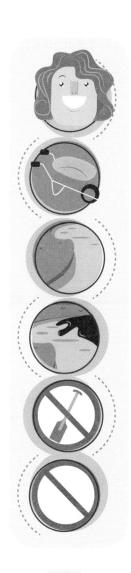

EXERCISE 1 Create your own story to help you remember the following:

   a. The Story Method

      Business Studies – What must be included on a food label?
Product name, producer, weight, price, best before, ingredients, origin, nutrients, cooking and storage instructions, barcode

_____

_____

_____

   b. History – New aids for navigation
Compass, log and line, astrolabe, quadrant, portolan charts

_____

_____

_____

 Learning Point 3

The Roman Room Method

If you're a fan of *Sherlock Holmes* you're probably already familiar with this method. This can be used to memorise huge volumes of information, and because it's all down to your imagination, you can constantly expand it.

This is how it works:

   a. Think of ten specific locations in your house that are on a path from the front door to another area of the house, like your bedroom; for example, the front door, picture on wall in hallway, kitchen table, dog's bed, fireplace in sitting room etc.

   b. Now write them down to remind you what places you chose.

   c. Now take your list of words that you need to remember and mentally place them one by one in the different locations. As you walk through the house, associate the word with the location using your imagination.

   d. To recall the information in an assessment, simply retrace your steps through the house and pick up each piece of information from where you left it down.

   e. When you want to add additional information to your memory bank, extend your journey, adding additional locations.

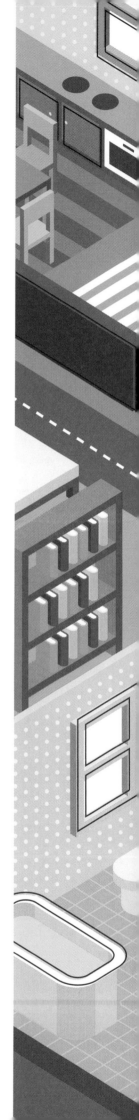

Note of interest: This must be a foolproof memory trick because it's been around since Greek and Roman times. The Roman orator Cicero, who needed to be able to recall large amounts of information from memory when giving speeches, described them in his treatise on oratory, *De Oratore*.

An example: In French, if you are trying to remember the vocabulary connected to weather.

You might mentally walk in through your front door and hang up your rain coat on the coat hook because 'il pluie'. Then go down the darkened hallway and see 'nuageux' reflected in the mirror. Go into the kitchen and take out your favourite coloured mug with an 'arc-en-ciel' on it. Go over to the window, look out at the tree swaying because it is 'venteux'.

Now take a journey through your own house and using the Roman Room method, try and memorise the various parts of the respiratory system:

The mouth and nose, pharynx (throat), larynx, trachea, bronchus, lungs, bronchioles, ribcages, intercostal muscles, diaphragm

EXERCISE 3   **a.** Write your locations and items to recall in the grid below.

Location Number	Location Description	Item to Remember
1		
2		
3		
4		
5		
6		
7		
8		
9		
10		

PAUSE AND REFLECT

1. What have you learned in this lesson?

_____

_____

2. How did you learn this?

_____

_____

3. How can you use what you learned in your schoolwork/study?

_____

_____

MENTAL NOTE

" Never stop dreaming, never stop believing, never give up, never stop trying, and never stop learning." – Roy T. Bennett, *The Light in the Heart*

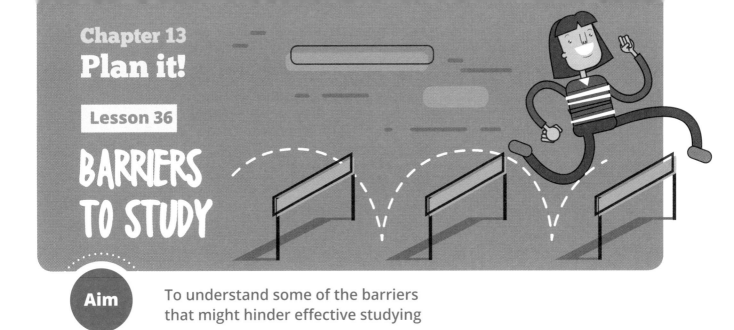

Aim   **To understand some of the barriers that might hinder effective studying**

 ## Learning Point 1

Now that you have explored the various elements of learning, the next step for you is to begin to look at study.

Assessment is a key part of the Junior Cycle and will be looked at in much more detail in the next section. However, it is important to note here that assessments are an integral part of the learning journey where you present what you have learned and you are given feedback to show how you may improve along with measuring your progress against your learning goals.

Study is what you do to help you prepare for these assessments. It is a systematic approach to going over everything you need to recall for your assessments.

 ## Learning Point 2

Most students tend to struggle when it comes to study so before you begin looking further at study let's explore some of the more common study barriers or difficulties that some students have.

Students when they are trying to study come up against some stumbling blocks or barriers. Some of these are real, which are called **conscious barriers**, and others are **subconscious**, which are not necessarily real. Regardless of what type of barrier or block it may be, simply identifying these barriers can help you overcome them because you then know what can be done.

EXERCISE 1

Conscious Barriers

Here is a list of some of the common physical barriers to effective studying. Can you think of any more and suggest any possible solutions?

a. Distractions, e.g. TV, busy social life

Other example

Solutions

b. Practical day-to-day reasons e.g. part-time job

Other example

Solutions

c. Physical study environment e.g. messy room

Other example

Solutions

d. Do you think any of these apply to you? ☐ Yes ☐ No

e. Which ones and what will you do about it?

EXERCISE 2

Subconscious Barriers

These can be even more powerful than the conscious barriers because these are your feelings. For each of the following feelings can you suggest possible ways this feeling may be lessened?

a. Anxiety about studying

b. Self-doubt about your ability

c. Fear of not doing well

d. Feeling overwhelmed by the amount of work

_____

e. Feeling pressured by teachers

_____

f. Just feeling stuck, not knowing what to do

_____

_____

g. Do you think any of these apply to you? ☐ **Yes** ☐ **No**

h. Which ones and what will you do about it?

_____

_____

_____

PAUSE AND REFLECT

1. What have you learned in this lesson?

_____

_____

2. How did you learn this?

_____

_____

3. How can you use what you learned in your schoolwork/study?

_____

_____

Chapter 13
Plan it!

Lesson 37

PLANNING YOUR STUDY

Aim To learn the importance of planning to succeed in learning

 Learning Point 1

In the last lesson you explored some of the barriers to effective study. The remaining chapters in this section introduce you to a simple study system which helps you become a more effective learner. The three simple steps to this study system are:

Plan it   **Do it**   **Review it**

 Learning Point 2

Let's begin with the first step, **PLAN IT**. When you were setting your goals you planned each action step that you needed to take along the way before you even began. **Planning is crucial to success**. If you want to be successful in your study you need to begin by planning what you need to do. Again, there are three steps to your planning:

(i)   Study goals

(ii)   Topics

(iii)   Timetable

EXERCISE 1

Step 1 Your Study Goals

Begin with looking at your study goals for the Junior Cycle. Try and answer the following questions as honestly as possible for yourself:

a. Do you want to do well in your learning? ☐ Yes ☐ No ☐ Not Sure

b. What does 'doing well' mean for you, what would it look like?

_____

_____

_____

If you know what you wish to achieve in each subject then you will be more likely to know how much effort you need to put into that subject.

For each of your subjects write down in the table that follows the grade you are aiming for from your summer assessments until your final exam. You will be able to look back at these to see if you are on target or not and be able to decide if any extra effort is needed.

Subject	Summer Assessments	Christmas	Mocks	Final Exam
Irish				
English				
Maths				
Science				
Geography				
History				
Business Studies				

Step 2 Topics

Being organised is a crucial element of being successful in your study. It is easier to study each subject if you break it down into its various topics; for example, you could begin to break history down into the following topics: • **The job of an historian** • **Ancient Rome** • **Medieval Life** etc. So for each subject break it down into its various topics. You now have a list of all the topics you need to study for each subject.

If you find this difficult go to your various subject teachers in the week ahead and ask them to help you as a class to identify the various topics for their subject. Over the next year as you complete topics in different subjects you can add them to your list.

EXERCISE 2 Your Study Journal

In Section 4 of this workbook you will find your *Study Journal*. There is a page for each subject where it can be broken into topics.

Write the name of one of your subjects on the top of each page and list the topics associated with this subject. You must do this for all your subjects.

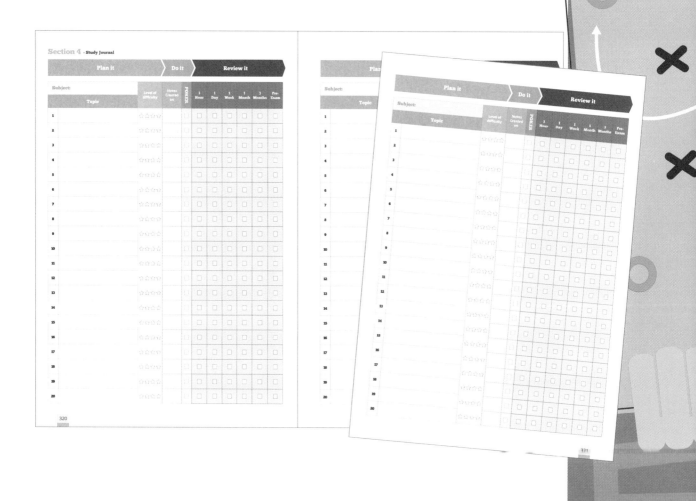

Step 3 Once you have this completed you know exactly what topics you need to study for your assessments. You will come back to looking at how you then use this page for your revision later on.

EXERCISE 3

Your Study Timetable

You have already had experience of writing out your class timetable, but have you considered creating a timetable for what you do with your time in the evenings and weekends? This should be your study timetable.

An effective study timetable has three elements:

a. **Detail** – everything you are doing each evening, not just study.

b. **Time** – the amount of time you will spend at each activity. It is recommended you spend half an hour at study per subject, then take a short break and begin with a new subject.

c. **Specific** – remember there is a difference between homework and study and also you have a number of subjects to study so include those as well.

Here is an example of a good study timetable for one day:

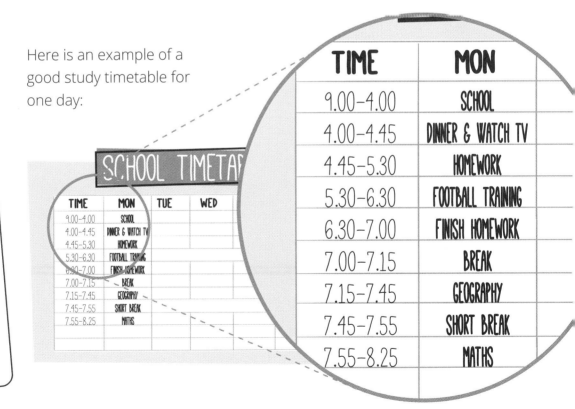

TIME	MON
9.00–4.00	SCHOOL
4.00–4.45	DINNER & WATCH TV
4.45–5.30	HOMEWORK
5.30–6.30	FOOTBALL TRAINING
6.30–7.00	FINISH HOMEWORK
7.00–7.15	BREAK
7.15–7.45	GEOGRAPHY
7.45–7.55	SHORT BREAK
7.55–8.25	MATHS

Each person has their own unique timetable as each person has different kinds of things going on in their lives. So now create your own study timetable for your week, where you are aiming to do at least **8 hours** broken into half hour slots of **study** between Monday and Friday and an extra **2.5 hours** between Saturday and Sunday.

Weekly Timetable

Time	MON	Time	TUE	Time	WED	Time	THU	Time	FRI	Time	SAT	Time	SUN

You can download sample timetables on **The Super Generation** website: **www.thesupergeneration.com**

PAUSE AND REFLECT

1. What have you learned in this lesson?

   _____

   _____

2. How did you learn this?

   _____

   _____

3. How can you use what you learned in your schoolwork/study?

   _____

   _____

MENTAL NOTE

"The more that you read, the more things you will know, the more you will learn, the more places you will go!" – Dr Seuss

Chapter 14
Do it!

Lesson 38

INTRODUCING POKER

Aim To introduce you to an effective study system

 **Learning Point 1**

Now that you have planned your study, the next step is to get on and do it! Smart study is not about the amount of time you spend but the quality of time you spend studying.

The most effective study notes are the ones you create yourself, as your memory will recall you actually going through the process. POKER enables you to create one-page summaries for each topic you have to study and a system to learn them.

POKER is a **mnemonic** to remember five words:

Pre-test, Overview, Key words, Etch it & sketch it, and Retest

Each time you complete a topic in class, you then apply your POKER system to create your one-page summary of notes.

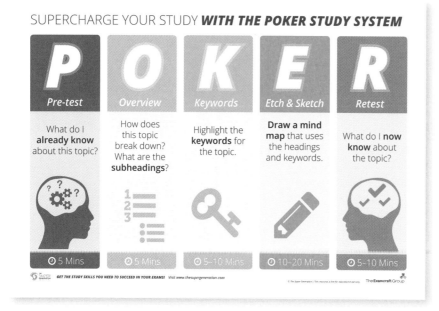

SUPERCHARGE YOUR STUDY **WITH THE POKER STUDY SYSTEM**

P	O	K	E	R
Pre-test	Overview	Keywords	Etch & Sketch	Retest
What do I **already know** about this topic?	How does this topic break down? What are the **subheadings**?	Highlight the **keywords** for the topic.	**Draw a mind map** that uses the headings and keywords.	What do I **now know** about the topic?
5 Mins	5 Mins	5–10 Mins	10–20 Mins	5–10 Mins

GET THE STUDY SKILLS YOU NEED TO SUCCEED IN YOUR EXAMS! Visit www.thesupergeneration.com

The Examcraft Group

DOWNLOAD
the PDF sample on
www.thesupergeneration.com

P – Pre-test

The following lessons will bring you through a worked example from the Junior Cycle History course and will look at the **Reformation**.

This exercise is about focusing the brain on what it is you need to study. This is an important step. When you sit down to study something the first thing you do is test yourself on what you know already. This not only saves you time but also primes your brain to look for the information you don't know. The best way to do that is to have a question in mind when you begin. Never start reading from the first page of the chapter. Look at the chapter summary first and see if there are any important questions and whether you can answer them. This should take no more than 5 minutes. You don't have to answer the questions completely.

So let's begin with the Pre-test. Here are your questions:

Junior Cycle History

a. Give two reasons why many people thought the Catholic Church was in need of reform around 1500.

b. In relation to Martin Luther, explain two of the following: 95 Theses, Papal Bull or Edict of Worms

c. From your study of the Reformation, give two differences between the beliefs of a named reformer and the beliefs of the Catholic Church.

d. In relation to Martin Luther, explain two of the following: Ireland, Britain or Mainland Europe

   Without reading ahead, in the box fill in everything you think you can recall to answer this question. Here is an example of some of the words you could write; do not try to put order on them at this stage.

Pre-test

Can you think of more?
Church abuses Power Martin Luther 95 theses Counter Reformation Seven sacraments

a. How well did you do?

(Good)   (Average)   (Can improve)

b. What does this tell you?

_____

_____

O – Overview

Once you have tested your knowledge, the next step is to get an overview of the topic. This is the big picture. You don't need to go into detail, you're trying to get the overall gist of the topic. What are the key ideas? What is important in the topic? What is not important? What information are they looking for to answer the question? You should spend no more than 5 minutes on this step. Scan over the text and identify the main subheadings, these provide the overview of the topic. You can put these in the box at the end of the text.

How does this topic break down? What are the **subheadings**?

1
2
3

5 Mins

The Reformation

What was the Reformation?

In the 16th century many people were unhappy with the way the Christian Church was managed. Some people left the Church in protest and set up new Protestant churches. This was called the Protestant Reformation because the new Protestants hoped to reform (improve) Christianity.

What caused the Reformation?

1. **Abuses in the Church**

    The Reformation was caused mainly by abuses (faults) in the Christian Church at the time.

    → **Ignorant Priests**

    Most priests were good and holy men who did their work very well. But some priests were ignorant. Many did not understand the Latin they used when saying Mass. More than 30 per cent of English priests did not even know the Ten Commandments of the Christian faith.

    → **Wealthy Bishops**

    Many bishops had become very wealthy, partly because of the money they got through tithes (church taxes) and partly because of money and land left by rich people to the Church. Some bishops seemed to show more interest in personal wealth than in serving their communities.

    → **Unworthy Popes**

    Some popes led unworthy or immoral lives. Pope Alexander VI, for example, had six mistresses and fathered several children.
    Pope Sixtus IV was involved in a failed plot to murder Lorenzo the Magnificent, the ruler of Florence.

2. **The Renaissance**

    The Renaissance helped to cause the Reformation.

    → *During the Renaissance, more people began to think for themselves and to question old ideas. This encouraged some people to criticise faults within the Church or even to leave the Church in protest against these faults.*

> ➔ *The Renaissance was also a time when popes spent huge amounts of money as patrons of the arts. Michelangelo's sculpture called the Pieta and his frescoes in the Sistine Chapel were examples of great art paid for by the Pope. But some of this money had been given to the Church as tithes paid by poor people. Many people were angry that the money of the poor should be used to pay for works of art.*

3. **The Printing Press**

The invention of printing caused the spread of new ideas. Some of these ideas were critical of the Church.

> ➔ *Martin Luther, the first Protestant, had his religious beliefs circulated widely through the printing press.*

> ➔ *The ideas of a Dutch monk named Erasmus were also circulated. Erasmus wrote a book called In Praise of Folly, in which he criticised abuses in the Church.*

Martin Luther – A Religious Reformer

Martin Luther (1483-1546) was born in the German state of Saxony. His father was a prosperous copper miner who reared Martin very strictly.

Martin became a student of law at Erfurt University. One day he was caught out in a frightening thunderstorm. He vowed that if his life were spared, he would become a monk. Shortly afterwards he joined the Augustinian order.

Father Luther became convinced that he (like almost everybody else) was a terrible sinner and that only faith in God could save his soul. This idea was called Justification by Faith.

While Luther was a well-known professor at the University of Wittenberg, Friar John Tetzel came to town offering indulgences in return for contributions to the rebuilding fund for St. Peter's Basilica in Rome. Luther was so angry that he printed his 95 theses against such practices and nailed them to the church door. Luther's theses (arguments) contradicted several church teachings.

Pope Leo X issued a papal bull condemning Luther. Then Emperor Charles V called a meeting of princes, known as the Diet of Worms. In the Edict of Worms, Luther was declared to be a heretic and an outlaw.

But Father Luther was protected by Frederick of Saxony in the prince's castle at Wartburg. While staying in the castle, Luther translated the Bible into German.

Luther's Protestant beliefs were laid out in a book called *The Confessions of Augsburg*. He believed, for example, that there were only two sacraments, Baptism and the Eucharist. He also believed that priests should be allowed to marry. He himself married an ex-nun named Catherine Von Bora.

Some princes supported Luther because he would give them control over the Church in their kingdoms. Others supported Luther because they disliked the abuses that then plagued the Catholic Church. Lutheranism therefore spread rapidly, especially in Northern Germany and in Scandinavia.

Results of the Reformation

1. A Divided Europe

The Reformation and Counter Reformation left Europe divided into Catholic and Protestant states. Southern Europe remained largely Catholic, while many countries in Northern Europe became Protestant.

2. Religious Wars

Religious divisions led or contributed to several wars in Europe.

→ *Soon after Martin Luther died in 1546, war broke out between Catholic and Lutheran princes in Germany. Neither side won. The war ended in 1555 with the Peace of Augsburg. Under this treaty, each prince was allowed to decide the religion of his people. As a result, most states in Northern Germany became Lutheran, whilst southern states remained Catholic.*

→ *An even more brutal religious conflict later broke out between Catholic and rotestant states in Northern Europe. This was the Thirty Years War, which took place between 1618 and 1648. It ended with the Treaty of Westphalia.*

→ *Catholic Spain and Protestant England went to war, partly because of their religious differences. This war included an attempted invasion of England in 1588 by a great Spanish fleet called the Armada.*

3. Religious Persecution

Many rulers thought that only people of the same religion as themselves could be loyal subjects. This is why Catholics were sometimes persecuted in Protestant countries such as England, while Protestants were sometimes persecuted in Catholic countries such as France.

4. Art and Architecture

Protestant churches were usually plain and simple in style. Catholic churches, on the other hand, followed Gothic or later Baroque styles. They were richly decorated with religious statues, paintings and stained glass windows.

5. Education

Education became more important as a result of the Reformation.

→ *Many Protestant leaders wanted all children to attend school so that they could learn to read the Bible for themselves. This is why there were many good schools in places such as John Calvin's Geneva.*

→ *Catholics also saw the importance of education in defending their religion against the spread of Protestantism. The Jesuits, for example, set up many good schools throughout the world.*

(New Complete History, Gill Education, Hayes, 2009)

O - Overview

Title: The Reformation

Subheadings:
What caused the Reformation?
Martin Luther - A Religious Reformer

K - Keywords

The next step is to go over the topic in detail and highlight the keywords that carry the most meaning. It is only at this stage you begin to read in detail. You can now fill in the keywords for each section/subheading below.

Fill in the table by continuing to read the remainder of the text on the Reformation and picking out the keywords from other sections.

K
Keywords

Highlight the **keywords** for the topic.

⏱ 5-10 Mins

Keywords

16th century protest,
Protestant Reformation

Abuses in church
> Ignorant priests, wealthy bishops,
   unworthy popes,
   Alexander VI, Sixtus IV
The Renaissance
> Think for themselves, patron
   of the arts, people angry, indulgences
Printing Press
> New ideas, Erasmus
> In praise of folly, Gutenberg Bible

Keywords

Have you noticed how quickly and easily you have already condensed the information you need to remember? This is what you call a one-page summary. So, rather than having pages and pages of notes, you have it all on one page in front of you.

PAUSE AND REFLECT

1. What have you learned in this lesson?

_____

_____

2. How did you learn this?

_____

_____

3. How can you use what you learned in your schoolwork/study?

_____

_____

MENTAL NOTE

"What you learn today, for no reason at all, will help
you discover all the wonderful secrets of tomorrow"
– Norton Juster, The Phantom Tollbooth

Do it!

Lesson 39

POKER 2

Aim   To introduce you to an effective study system

Learning Point 1

This lesson follows on from the previous one, where you learned to create an effective one-page summary. You have previously learned that the two important keys to your memory are imagination and association. You are now going to apply these to your notes to aid your memory.

....

Learning Point 2

E – Etch & Sketch

The **Etch & Sketch** section is where you create your notes — your one-page summaries - and then etch them into your memory. You will recall in Chapter 12 on memory you looked at some simple techniques to help you memorise information.

Likewise, when you begin to go to the effort of creating your own notes, your brain will recall this action. When making notes on any topic it's important that you try to put all the information for that topic on one page. It's much easier for the brain to see all the information on a topic on one page and to see how all the relevant elements are connected.

You have already created a one-page summary in the last lesson, where you listed all the keywords under each heading in the text. This is what a lot of people do. But we want you to be more efficient in your study by creating a mind map, which is a visual one-page summary.

Etch & Sketch

Draw a mind map that uses the headings and keywords.

⏱ 10–20 Mins

One-page Summary

Let's begin by re-creating your one-page summary in a slightly different format. Take your list of subheadings and keywords and write them out in different colours for each section/subheading. You should be able to put them all on one page.

The Reformation

16th century protest,
Protestant Reformation

Abuses in church
> Ignorant priests, wealthy
   bishops, unworthy popes,
   Alexander VI, Sixtus IV

The Renaissance
> Think for themselves, patron
   of the arts, people angry,
   indulgences

Printing Press
> New ideas, Erasmus
> In praise of folly,
        Gutenberg Bible

Have you noticed how much brighter and more pleasant this is to the brain than black or blue ink?

Quickly, how many sections have you? _____

Did you count the number of coloured sections or did you count the number of subheadings? _____

Most people would count the number of coloured sections as they stand out more. Keeping each section in one colour also begins to add structure to your notes.

Images

Quick test for you, if I was to say the word elephant to you would you see the word e-l-e-p-h-a-n-t or an image of an elephant in your mind? Most people would see the image of the elephant as we tend to visualise images rather than words. Images help us remember things more easily. You are now going to create images for your subheadings and keywords.

When you try to create an associated image for a word the brain will remember not only the image but the associated memory of trying to come up with an image. The image does not need to be the word itself but could be anything that will help you remember the word. Try and create images for the following keywords you might have had in your list.

Priests

Bishops

Renaissance

Printing press

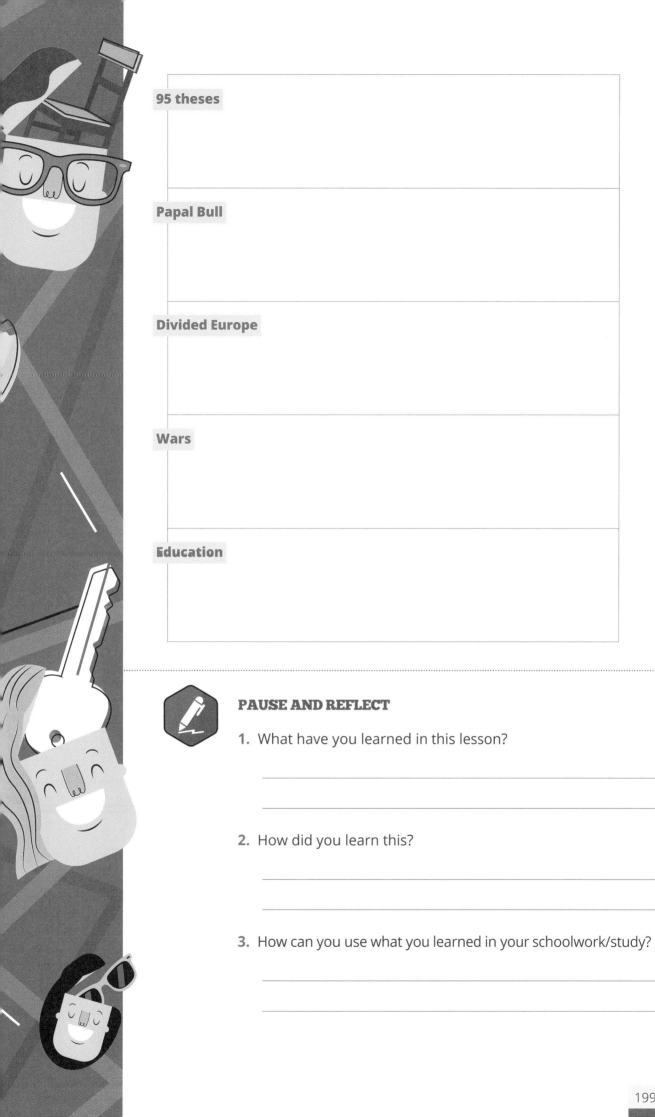

95 theses	
Papal Bull	
Divided Europe	
Wars	
Education	

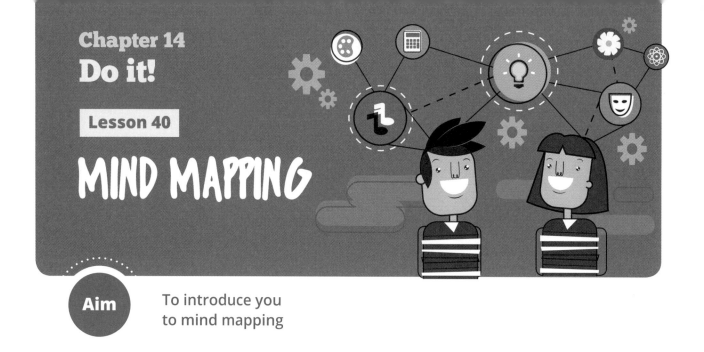

MIND MAPPING

Aim — To introduce you to mind mapping

 Learning Point 1

If the brain understands something, this means it is able to see how the various elements or pieces of information are all connected and come together. If we understand something then it is easier to remember that piece of information. That is why mind maps are so powerful, because they reflect graphically how all the information for a particular topic is woven together using your keywords and images.

 Learning Point 2

A mind map is a diagram which you can use to visually organise the information in your notes. A mind map is hierarchical, which means it shows the order of importance of various pieces of information and how they are related to each other as a whole. There are seven golden rules to follow when you create a mind map:

(i) Use either blank A4 or preferably A3 paper in landscape so you have plenty of space to fill in all the information.

(ii) Start with a central image representing what the topic is about.

(iii) Use smaller images throughout to help you remember the keywords or concepts.

(iv) Draw branches from the central image to create a structure. The branches should be the same length and colour as the text. The text should be on the branches.

(v) Only use keywords, do not write whole sentences or bullet points. Print your keywords clearly.

(vi) Connect everything up. Everything should be connected by the branches back to the central image. Nothing should be on its own on the map.

(vii) Have fun. Use your imagination and creativity as much as possible, especially with the images. Your brain will enjoy creating something like this much more than writing out pages and pages of notes.

Below is a mind map of the **Golden Rules** of goal mind-mapping.

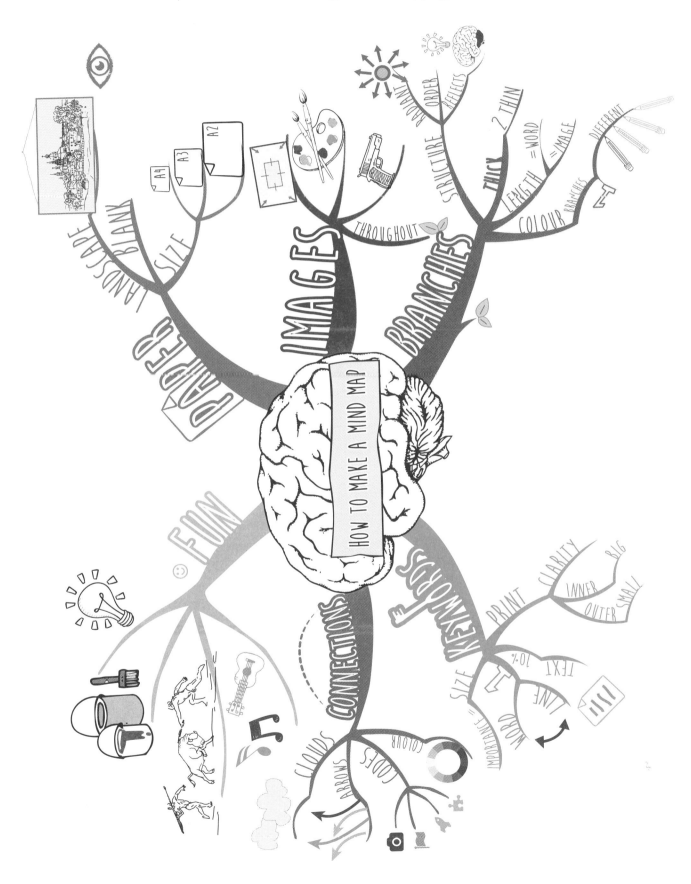

EXERCISE 1

Mind Map Rules

Having read through the rules and looking at the mind map try and answer these simple questions on what a mind map is.

a. What type of paper do you use?

b. Ideally what size and layout should it be?

c. Where are the branches thickest?

d. Why do you think they get slimmer as you move out from the central image?

e. How long should the branches be?

f. How many colours do you use on each branch?

g. Answer True or False for the following:

Only images are used.	☐ True	☐ False
Only bullet points are used.	☐ True	☐ False
Only keywords are used.	☐ True	☐ False
You only use one colour for everything.	☐ True	☐ False
Keywords and images are used throughout.	☐ True	☐ False
There is no need to connect everything together.	☐ True	☐ False
You write the keywords at the end of each branch.	☐ True	☐ False

h. Which do you think your brain would prefer spending time on, writing out pages of notes or creating a colourful mind map by following the POKER system?

EXERCISE 2 — Mind Map Rules 2

Now that you know a little bit more about mind maps do you think you can fill in the blanks on the following Rules of Mind Maps using the words below?

branches	fun	colour	central	blank
image	landscape	keywords	images	

Rule 1: Use ( ) paper in ( ) format.

Rule 2: Start with a ( ) ( ).

Rule 3: Use ( ) only.

Rule 4: Use ( ) everywhere.

Rule 5: Use ( ) throughout.

Rule 6: Use ( ) to connect.

Rule 7: Have ( ).

EXERCISE 3 — Which is Better? Why?

Which do you think is better for helping you memorise and recall information when you go to revise?

a. Pages of bullet point notes

b. A one-page summary

c. A mind map.

Explain your answer:

_____

_____

EXERCISE 4 — Reformation Mind Map

Now that you know the rules of mind mapping and have already broken down your topic on the Reformation to its subheadings and keywords, you can draw your own mind map, either on this page or on a blank A3 page.

Remember your **Golden Rules** as you are drawing.

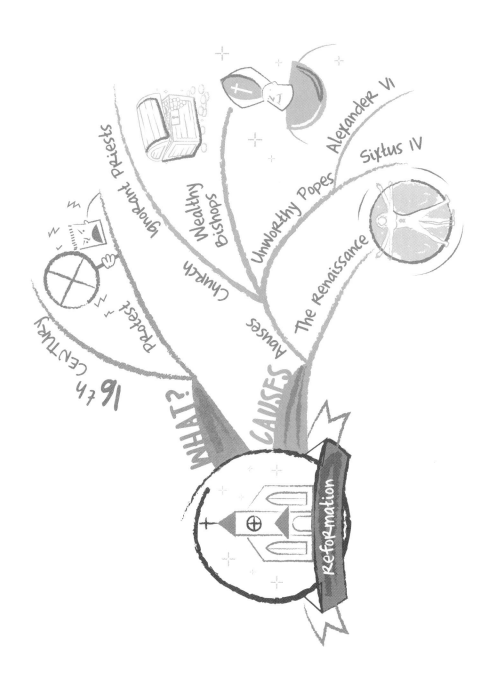

Ignorant Priests

Wealthy Bishops

Church

Unworthy Popes

Alexander VI

Sixtus IV

The Renaissance

Abuses

Protest

16th CENTURY

WHAT?

CAUSES

Reformation

Etch

Now that you have created your mind map as a one-page summary, let's go back and practise some of our simple memory techniques to etch some of the information contained into your memory.

Try the following exercises:

a. Can you come up with a simple acronym that you could use to help you remember the various subheadings in the text on the Reformation?

_____

_____

b. Can you think of a silly sentence that will help you remember the causes of the Reformation?

_____

_____

Don't forget that etching is important for helping you recall important pieces of information from your notes. You should try and use regularly some of the various memory techniques you have already learned each time you create your notes.

PAUSE AND REFLECT

1. What have you learned in this lesson?

_____

_____

2. How did you learn this?

_____

_____

3. How can you use what you learned in your schoolwork/study?

_____

_____

Aim To encourage you to create your own mind maps

 **Learning Point 1**

R - Retest

R

Retest

What do I **now know** about the topic?

⏱ 5–10 Mins

The last step of POKER after Pre-Test, Overview, Keyword and Etch & Sketch is Retest.

You should always end your study sessions with a little test to check what you have learned. You now have your study notes from your topic and you are going to spend 5-10 minutes retesting yourself on what you know about the topic. You turn over all your notes, take out a blank piece of paper and write/draw/say everything you now know on the topic. Remember, you are studying in order to be able to recall – the more you train your brain to recall what you have learned the higher the chance that you will be able to recall it when you need it for assessment purposes.

 EXERCISE 1 So let's see what you can recall from your study session. Take out your question again and try and write down everything you know. It has already been started here for you as an example.

a. Give two reasons why many people thought the Catholic Church was in need of reform around 1500:

Abuses in the Church > ignorant priests, wealthy bishops,

unworthy popes, indulgences

Printing press > Gutenberg Bible, Erasmus, In Praise of Folly

b. In relation to Martin Luther, explain two of the following:
   95 Theses, Papal Bull or Edict of Worms.

   Papal Bull > Pope Leo 1520, condemned Luther's ideas, Luther

   burned a copy, excommunicated

   Edict of Worms > German princes ruled by Emperor Charles V,

   summoned meeting at Worms, issued Diet of Worms, condemned

   Luther as outlaw, fled to Wartburg Castle, protected by

   Frederick of Saxony

Can you complete the rest?

c. From your study of the Reformation, give two differences
   between the beliefs of a named reformer and the beliefs
   of the Catholic Church in:

   (i) Ireland:

   (ii) Britain:

   (iii) Mainland
         Europe:

d. Write an account of the impact of the Reformation on two
   of the following:

   (i) Ireland:

   (ii) Britain:

   (iii) Mainland
         Europe:

EXERCISE 2

Retest

Now that you have completed your mind map one-page summary, you can turn it over, look at your question again and see if you can now answer the question.

a. How did you do?

_____

_____

b. Do you feel you understand the topic much better now? Don't worry if you didn't remember everything, that will come with your regular review or revision of the topic.

_____

_____

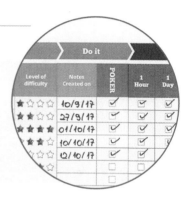

Once you have completed this step, your study session is over. You can now go to your **Study Journal** Subject Study Planner at the back of the workbook. Go to the 'Do It' section, write the date and tick the POKER box next to the topic you have studied.

PAUSE AND REFLECT

1. What have you learned in this lesson?

_____

_____

2. How did you learn this?

_____

_____

3. How can you use what you learned in your schoolwork/study?

_____

_____

MENTAL NOTE

" All the world is a laboratory to
the inquiring mind." – Martin H. Fischer

Chapter 15
POKER Practice

Lesson 42
STUDYING LANGUAGES

Aim To provide you with the opportunity to practise POKER

 Learning Point 1

The next few lessons are an opportunity for you to practise what you have just learned using the POKER system and apply it to the variety of subjects you are studying for the Junior Cycle. One of the best ways to embed any learning and skill development is practice and this is simply what the next few lessons are about.

 EXERCISE 1

Languages

POKER and mind maps work really well for studying Irish and modern languages. For languages, you are expected to learn a broad vocabulary in relation to certain topics or themes, such as yourself, your home, locality etc.

Let's study Mé Féin for Irish or use the topic 'Myself' from another language.

 Pre-test

Overview: (Hint: subheadings would be Cur síos, Mo theaghlach, Caithimh aimsire or description, my family, hobbies)

Keywords

R **Retest**

···

EXERCISE 2 You can also use this for studying the various aspects of grammar.
Let's study your verbs for one of the modern languages you are studying.

P **Pre-test** (Hint: the different types of verbs)

O **Overview:** (Hint: regular/irregular or past, present, future)

K **Keywords**

R **Retest**

PAUSE AND REFLECT

1. What have you learned in this lesson?

   _____

   _____

2. How did you learn this?

   _____

   _____

3. How can you use what you learned in your schoolwork/study?

   _____

   _____

Chapter 15
POKER Practice

Lesson 43

STUDYING ENGLISH

 Aim To provide you with the opportunity to practise POKER

 Learning Point 1

You looked at how POKER can be used for studying other languages, but it is also really useful for creating one-page summaries for the various elements of literature in English. You can create a one-page summary for a play, short story, novel, poem etc. What you do is simply create branches for the characters, plot development, themes, techniques etc.

 EXERCISE 1 **Drama/Novel/Short Story**

You will need your English text book for this exercise and will need to choose a story you have studied in class.

Title of Short Story:

_____

 Pre-test (a brief summary)

Overview: (identify key elements i.e. characters, plot etc.)

 Keywords

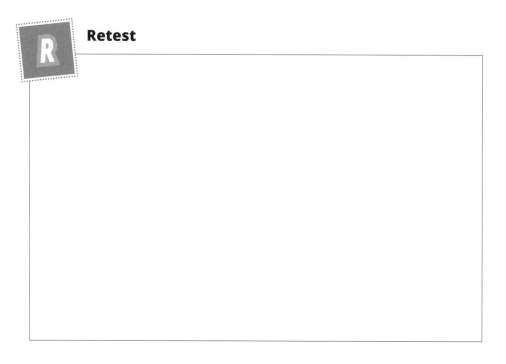

Retest

EXERCISE 2

Poetry

Here is a sample poetry question for you.

Choose a poem you have studied in which the poet has something interesting to say about the relationship between either people and nature or adults and children.

(a) Describe the relationship dealt with in your chosen poem and explain why you find this relationship interesting.

(b) How does the poet's use of either sounds or images in your chosen poem help you to understand what the poet feels about the relationship? Explain your answer with reference to the poem.

Title of Poem:

Pre-test (a brief summary)

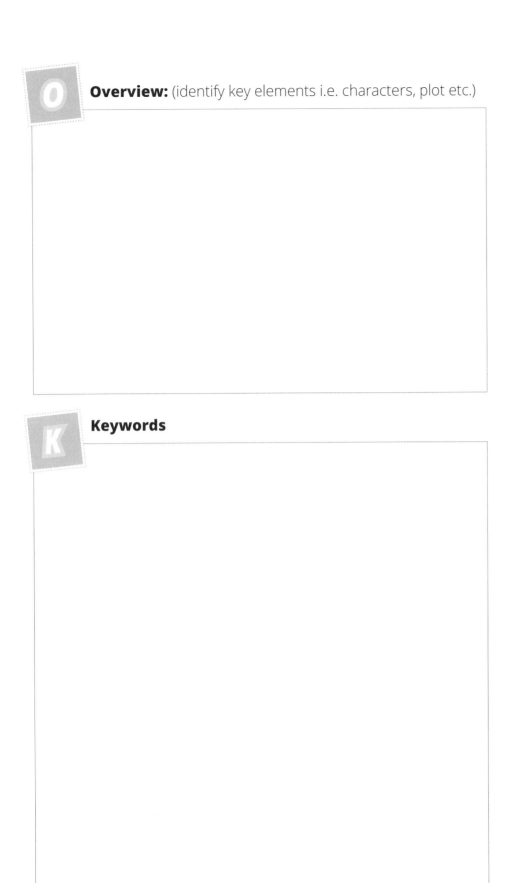

Overview: (identify key elements i.e. characters, plot etc.)

Keywords

Etch & Sketch

Retest

PAUSE AND REFLECT

1. What have you learned in this lesson?

_____

_____

2. How did you learn this?

_____

_____

3. How can you use what you learned in your schoolwork/study?

_____

_____

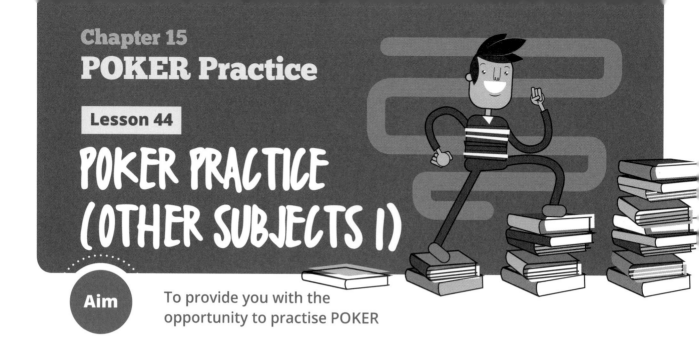

Chapter 15
POKER Practice

Lesson 44

POKER PRACTICE (OTHER SUBJECTS 1)

Aim To provide you with the opportunity to practise POKER

 Learning Point 1

Practice makes perfect. These lessons will give you the opportunity to practise POKER in other subjects. You will need your text books to help you.

EXERCISE 1 **Business Studies – Economic Growth**
Try this question from the Business Studies course:

a. Ireland continues to have the fastest economic growth in the EU.

(i) Explain the term 'economic growth'.

(ii) Identify the official measure of economic growth in Ireland.

(iii) Explain two economic implications for Ireland's economy from this improvement in economic growth.

(iv) What do the initials EU stand for?

(v) How many countries, including Ireland, make up the EU?

b. In any economy, factors of production are required to produce goods and services. Explain the four factors of production and the reward/payment associated with each.

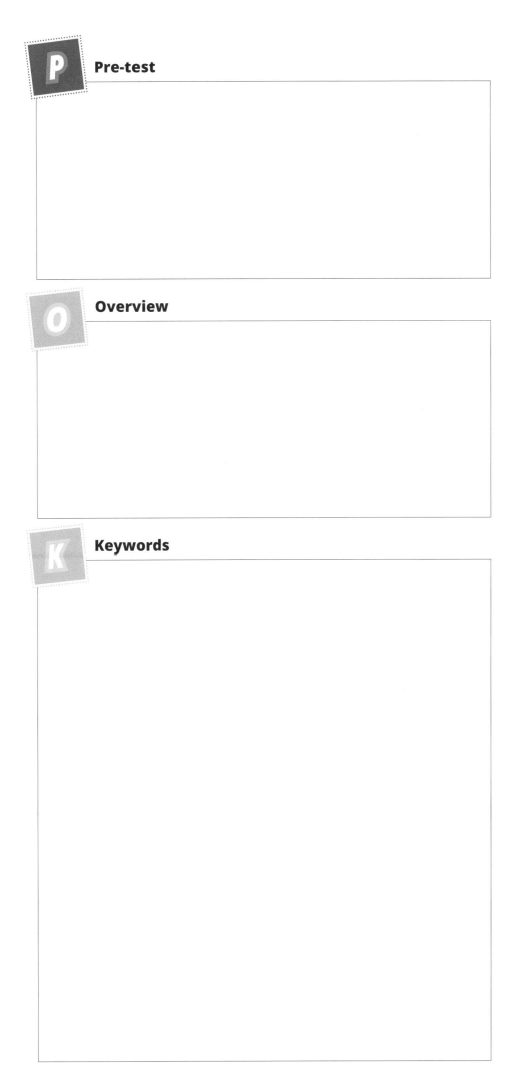

Pre-test

Overview

Keywords

Etch & Sketch

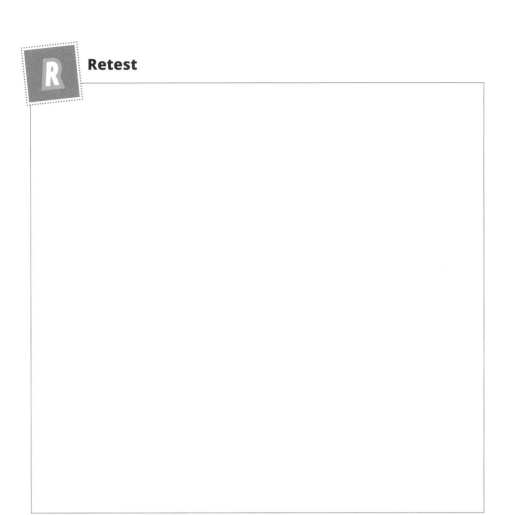

Retest

PAUSE AND REFLECT

1. What have you learned in this lesson?

_____

_____

2. How did you learn this?

_____

_____

3. How can you use what you learned in your schoolwork/study?

_____

_____

MENTAL NOTE

" The only person who is educated is the one who has
learned how to learn ... and change." – Carl Rogers

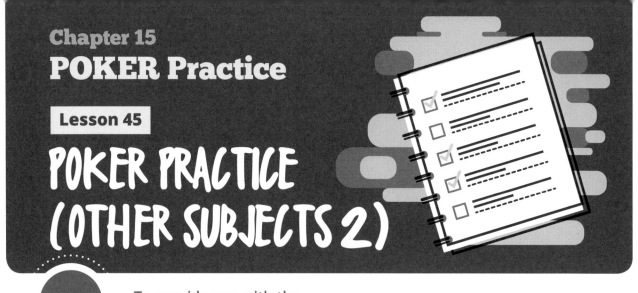

Lesson 45

POKER PRACTICE (OTHER SUBJECTS 2)

Aim — To provide you with the opportunity to practise POKER

 Learning Point 1

Further practice on the POKER system from Science

 Science – Cells

Try this question from the Science course.

a. All living things are made of cells. The diagram is of an animal cell.

(i) Name the part labelled X.

(ii) Name one substance that is able to pass through the membrane of an animal cell.

b. Plant cells are grouped into tissues.

(i) Name one example of a plant tissue

(ii) State the function of the plant tissue you have named.

c. In germinating seeds, the radicle always grows downwards.

(i) What name is given to this growth response?

(ii) What is the advantage to the plant of the radicle always growing downwards?

P Pre-test

O Overview

K Keywords

Etch & Sketch

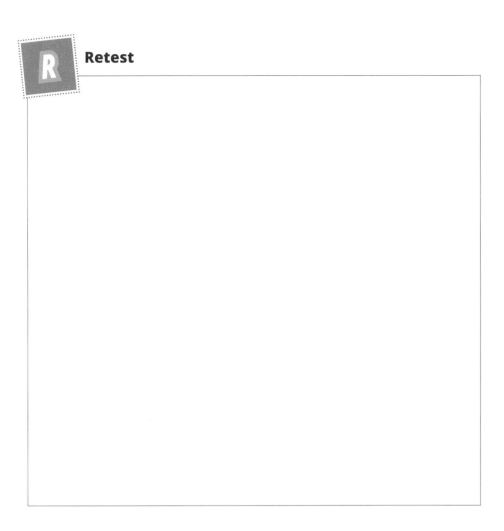

Retest

PAUSE AND REFLECT

1. What have you learned in this lesson?

_____

_____

2. How did you learn this?

_____

_____

3. How can you use what you learned in your schoolwork/study?

_____

_____

Chapter 16
Review it!

Lesson 46

PLANNING AND EXECUTING REVISION

Aim To learn the importance of revision and how to organise your revision

 Learning Point 1

Now that you have learned how to do it, i.e. how to study by creating your own notes and using your memory techniques, the next step is to Review it. This final step looks at revision and the importance of regular review.

 Learning Point 2

In lesson 36 you learned about the 'Forgetting curve' – how you forget up to 90% of the information you take in within a week if you do not revisit or look at that information again.

However, there is a very simple review system which you can use to help achieve MAXIMUM recall. It is called the **5 x 5 Review** and works like this:

When you create your notes on a topic you put them aside and then

After one hour | One day | One week | One month | Three months

you simply take them out and read over them.

By following this simple process you will change your 'forgetting curve' into a **'memory curve'**, where you will be able to recall up to **96%** of what you have read.

It looks like this:

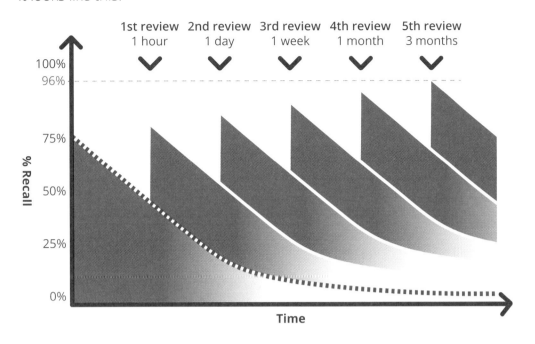

% Recall / Time

1st review — 1 hour
2nd review — 1 day
3rd review — 1 week
4th review — 1 month
5th review — 3 months

Learning Point 3

Hopefully at this stage you realise how important organisation is. You would have looked at your revision study planner when you were planning and again when you were doing your study.

Do you remember your study journal at the end of the workbook where you filled in a page for each subject and its topics? Well now you are going to use those pages to help you organise and record your revision.

Planning Your Reviews

Go to your study journal and look at your list of topics for each subject. Take your list of topics and STAR rate the topics according to how DIFFICULT they may be.

Do this now for three subjects of your choice – give star ratings to the topics you already have there.

Each student has their own star rating per topic. These ratings can help you manage study much more efficiently. You can decide to do a couple of easy topics on days you are tired, have hobbies or other commitments. You can do harder topics on days you are freer and may have better concentration. The key is to know that study is a piecemeal exercise, little pieces of work over a long period of time, not cramming or one giant effort at the end.

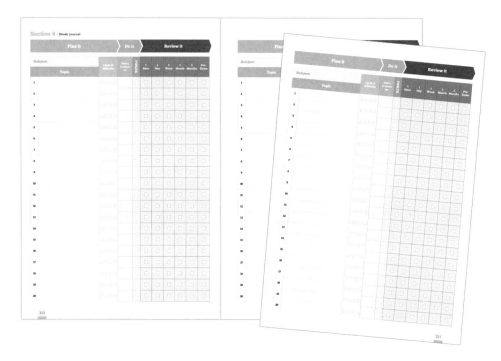

Finally, you will notice the **5 x 5 Review** system along the top of each page, do not forget to check these off every time you revise a topic.

In this way you have a clear outline of what you have revised and what needs revising in each subject.

Advantages of Revision

Here is a list of statements about the advantages of revision. For each of the statements decide whether it is true or false and explain your answer.

a. You are likely to be more relaxed when you revise regularly.
☐ True ☐ False

Explain:
_____

_____

b. You rediscover interesting material that you might have forgotten about in a topic. ☐ True ☐ False

Explain:
_____

_____

c. Going over material several times at regular intervals helps to build recall of it. ☐ True ☐ False

Explain:
_____

_____

d. You feel more confident about your subjects the more you revise. ☐ True ☐ False

Explain:

e. When you study regularly you begin to make the connections between the various elements of a topic and the topics to the overall subject. ☐ True ☐ False

Explain:

f. You identify areas that you might need some extra assistance with when you revise. ☐ True ☐ False

Explain:

g. When you study you feel you are making progress in your study and learning. ☐ True ☐ False

Explain:

PAUSE AND REFLECT

1. What have you learned in this lesson?

2. How did you learn this?

3. How can you use what you learned in your schoolwork/study?

Chapter 16
Review it!

YOUR APPROACH TO REVISION

Aim To explore with you your own attitude and approach to revising

 **Learning Point 1**

Now that you know what revision is about and how to organise your revision you can use this lesson to reflect on your own approaches to revision and how you can avoid some of the common pitfalls that students face when it comes to revision.

EXERCISE 1 **Attitudes and Approaches to Revision**

Let's take a moment to explore some of the common pitfalls students face when they are revising.

a. On a scale of 1 to 10, how good do you think you are at revising, where 1 is not good at all and 10 is excellent?

| 1 | 2 | 3 | 4 | 5 | 6 | 7 | 8 | 9 | 10 |

b. Give a reason for your answer.

c. Read the study pitfalls below and place a tick in the box that you think is the most appropriate for you.

Common Pitfalls	Never	Sometimes	Often	A lot
Creating notes but never looking over them				
Avoiding revision because you find it boring				
Leaving revision to the last minute				
Spending more time revising the subjects you like most				
Spending a lot of time planning but not following through				
Allowing yourself to be distracted by your mobile or music				
Trying to revise too much at once and not being able to remember what you revised				
Always finding something more important that can be done.				

d. Having completed the exercise above, rate your ability to revise on a scale of 1 to 10, where 1 is not good at all and 10 is excellent.

1   2   3   4   5   6   7   8   9   10

e. Did your answer change?   ☐ Yes ☐ No

f. Why?

_____

_____

_____

EXERCISE 2

Possible Solutions

Now that you have identified some of the common pitfalls, can you match some of the possible solutions to the particular pitfall? From the list choose which you think are possible solutions to the pitfalls, and write them in the box opposite the pitfall.

Possible solutions:

a. Create a detailed study planner so you know what subject you are revising each night.

b. Turn off your phone and other devices during study time.

c. Set yourself a limit of half an hour per subject.

d. Record what topics you have revised and how often.

e. Test yourself before you begin revising to focus your mind.

f. Stick to your planned study timetable.

g. Don't make more than three changes to your study timetable.

h. Plan your revision out over a number of months.

i. Set yourself clear objectives for what you want to revise each night.

j. Vary how you revise; you might decide to read aloud rather than silently.

k. Test yourself at the end of a revision session to see what you remember.

l. Vary subjects each night between those you enjoy most and least.

m. Allow yourself short breaks so you do not get over tired.

n. Clean up your study environment before you begin your revision.

Some of the pitfalls might have more than one solution so some solutions may be repeated in your answers.

Common Pitfalls	Possible Solutions
Creating notes but never looking over them	
Avoiding revision because you find it boring	
Leaving revision to the last minute	
Spending more time revising the subjects you like most	
Spending a lot of time planning but not following through	
Allowing yourself to be distracted by your mobile or music	
Trying to revise too much at once and not being able to remember what you revised	
Always finding something more important that can be done.	

EXERCISE 2

Can you think of a possible solution to any of the pitfalls that isn't mentioned?

_____

_____

_____

Share with your class, it could possibly really help your friends with their revision.

Learning Point 2

Here again are your simple steps to effective studying:

i.   Plan it!

ii.   Do it!

iii.   Review it!

PAUSE AND REFLECT

1. What have you learned in this lesson?

_____

_____

2. How did you learn this?

_____

_____

3. How can you use what you learned in your schoolwork/study?

_____

_____

MENTAL NOTE

"I hear and I forget. I see and I remember.
I do and I understand." – Confucius

END OF SECTION REFLECTION

 Now that you have completed the second section of this programme, let's pause and reflect on all that you have learned.

In this section you will look at:

→ Reflecting on the Junior Cycle key skills which you developed

→ Exploring what you enjoyed most or least and why

→ Identifying how you used what you learned in other areas of your studies

→ Identifying possible areas you would like to focus on in the future.

Use the table below to rate your learning and performance from this section. Remember when considering your answers to reflect on all the variety of activities you engaged in during this section.

Managing Myself

1 Poor   **2** Fair   **3** Good   **4** Very Good   **5** Excellent

Key Skills		Student rating	Briefly Explain
Knowing myself			
I can ...	Recognise my personal strengths and weaknesses		
	Identify influences that make me who I am		
	Express my opinion		
Making considered decisions			
I can ...	Consider different options and ideas		
	Make plans and organise my work		
	Explain my choices to others		
Setting and achieving personal goals			
I can ...	Set personal goals		
	Identify what I need in order to achieve my goals		
	Ask for help when needed		
	Prepare detailed plans		
	Learn from my past actions and make changes if necessary		

Key Skills		Student rating	Briefly Explain
Being able to reflect on my learning			
I can ...	Evaluate and reflect on my learning		
	Receive and give feedback on my learning		
	Assess my own learning and suggest ways that I can improve		

Staying Well

1 Poor   **2** Fair   **3** Good   **4** Very Good   **5** Excellent

Key Skills		Student rating	Briefly Explain
Being confident			
I can ...	Communicate my opinions and beliefs with confidence in a variety of ways		
	Contribute to decision making within the class and group		

Key Skills		Student rating	Briefly Explain
Being positive about learning			
I can ...	Find enjoyment and fun in learning		
	Learn from my mistakes and move on		
	Stick with things and work them through until I succeed		
	Recognise and celebrate my achievements		

Communicating

1 Poor   **2** Fair   **3** Good   **4** Very Good   **5** Excellent

Key Skills		Student rating	Briefly Explain
Listening and expressing myself			
I can ...	Listen actively		
	Express what I think and feel clearly in an appropriate tone		
	Agree and disagree respectfully		
	Ask well-thought-out questions and listen to the answer		
	Use different styles of communication		
Performing and presenting			
I can ...	Express my ideas through presentation such as design and graphics		
	Make choices about how I can best present my ideas to others		
Discussing and debating			
I can ...	Participate confidently in class discussion		
	Present my point of view and be able to explain and support it		
	Respond to opposite arguments constructively		
Using numbers and data			
I can ...	Present, interpret and compare information using charts/diagrams.		

Key Skills		Student rating	Briefly Explain
Using language			
I can ...	Understand and use a wide vocabulary		
	Edit, correct and improve my written work		
	Use a range of forms to express my ideas.		

Being Creative

1 Poor **2** Fair **3** Good **4** Very Good **5** Excellent

Key Skills		Student rating	Briefly Explain
Imagining			
I can ...	Use different ways of learning to help develop my imagination		
Exploring options and alternatives			
I can ...	Think through a problem step-by-step		
	Try different approaches when working on a task		
	Seek out different viewpoints and consider them carefully		
	Repeat the whole exercise if necessary		
Implementing ideas and taking action			
I can ...	See things through to completion		
	Evaluate different ideas		
Learning creatively			
I can ...	Participate in learning in creative ways		
	Suggest creative ways that help me to learn		

Working with Others

① Poor   **②** Fair   **③** Good   **④** Very Good   **⑤** Excellent

Key Skills		Student rating	Briefly Explain
Developing good relationships and dealing with conflict			
I can ...	Share my ideas honestly		
	Show respect for different points of view		
	Give and receive praise and criticism constructively		
Co-operating			
I can ...	Show appreciation for the contribution of other group members		
	Contribute to decisions as part of a group		
Learning with others			
I can ...	Work in pairs and larger groups to help each other when we are learning		
	Help other students to understand and solve problems		
	Recognise that others can support my learning and know how to get their support		

Managing Information and Thinking

① Poor **②** Fair **③** Good **④** Very Good **⑤** Excellent

Key Skills		Student rating	Briefly Explain
I can ...	Look for new and different ways of answering questions and solving problems		
	Ask questions to probe more deeply		

Gathering, recording, organising and evaluating information and data			
I can ...	Recognise what I already know		
	Prepare and organise information and data so it makes sense to me and others		

Thinking creatively and critically			
I can ...	Question ideas and assumptions		
	Make connections between what I already know and new information		
	Adjust my thinking in light of new information		

Reflecting on and evaluating my learning			
I can ...	Reflect on and review my own progress		
	Identify barriers to my learning and suggest ways of overcoming them		
	Use a range of tools to help manage my learning		
	Keep believing that with continued effort I can succeed.		

1. Name three things you learned in this section?

   a. _____

   b. _____

   c. _____

2. What three things did you enjoy the most in this section?

   a. _____

   b. _____

   c. _____

   Why did you enjoy these?

   _____

   _____

3. Outline the three things which you found most difficult or challenging.

   a. _____

   b. _____

   c. _____

4. Name three things you have taken from this section and have begun to use in your other subjects.

   a. _____

   b. _____

   c. _____

NOTES

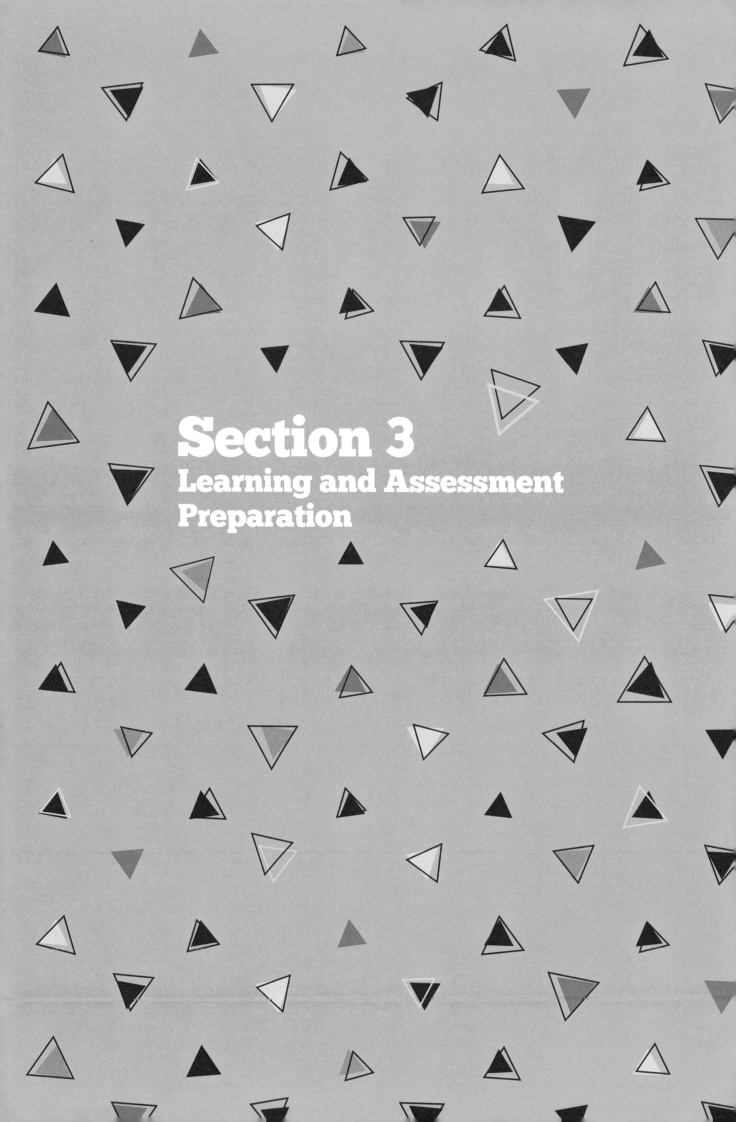

Section 3
Learning and Assessment Preparation

Introduction

In this last section of your programme you will explore some of the strategies that will enable you to achieve and succeed.

This section focuses on preparing you for assessments. You will explore the purpose and different types of assessment.

Some people find that simply being assessed and having to do assessments can be quite stressful and even upsetting. In this section you explore some simple strategies that can help you cope with this pressure. You also get tips to help you prepare for any assessment or examination.

This section is broken down into three key areas:

- **Chapters 17** Along with looking at the variety of assessments you come across in the Junior Cycle, this chapter also explores the purpose of assessments, their benefit and how you can use the feedback to aid you in your learning.

- **Chapters 18 and 19** look at how you can develop resilience as a learner, become more confident along with exploring some strategies to help you cope with the stress of learning and assessments.

- Finally, **Chapter 20** looks at how to prepare yourself properly for any examination, by taking another look at your revision practices and sharing with you tips that help you in the days before, the day of and in the examination itself.

Section 3
Learning and Assessment Preparation

Chapter 17
Assessment and Feedback

Chapter 18
Resilience

Chapter 19
Coping with Stress

Chapter 20
Preparation for Assessment

End of Section Reflection

Lesson 48

ASSESSMENT, WHAT IS IT ALL ABOUT?

Aim To help you understand the importance and relevance of assessments

 Learning Point 1

In the last section you learned about study and how study is preparation for assessments. So in the next few lessons you will look at what assessments are all about.

Assessments, whether you like them or not, are a key element to your learning journey. Assessment is about gathering evidence of knowledge learned or skills developed for the purposes of:

(i) Giving you feedback on your learning.

(ii) Identifying and showing you some areas where you could improve your learning

(iii) Providing you with a way of measuring your progress against the goals that you set for yourself.

 Learning Point 2

During the Junior Cycle you will come across a variety of assessment activities, which can be divided into two categories. These are:

(i) **Formative assessment:** This type of assessment *for learning* is where feedback is given to you on an ongoing basis so you can make adjustments and improve. Formative assessments normally occur during class or as pieces of homework and usually occur quite regularly.

   The teacher explains to you how well you are doing in your learning and identifies ways in which you can improve.

(ii) **Summative assessment:** This can be referred to as assessment *of learning*, marking the end of a particular phase of learning. It records a snapshot in time telling you, your teacher and your parents how well you have completed the learning tasks and activities, providing a formal reporting structure.

In the next exercise you will explore a variety of assessments that occur regularly during the Junior Cycle.

Assessment Activities

→ Read through the list of assessment activities below and categorise each activity into either formative or summative in the table that follows: **worksheets, oral questioning from teacher, project work, homework exercises, presentations, class quiz, investigations, projects, end of term exams, end of learning cycle exams, essays**.

Formative assessment	Summative assessment

If you can think of other assessment activities add them to your list above. If you are unsure about what some of the activities are you can ask your teacher to explain them to you.

 Learning Point 3

Along with providing feedback to you for your learning and on your learning, there are also many other benefits to assessment, including:

(i) They increase your motivation.

(ii) They provide evidence of what you have learned and achieved.

(iii) They help you work to your strengths.

(iv) They can help predict your future potential.

(v) They demonstrate your mastery of new skills.

EXERCISE 2

What are the Benefits?

At this stage of your learning journey you will already have encountered many of the various activities. Read through the list of benefits again in learning point 2 and see if you are able to think of examples that could prove each of the benefits.

Benefit	How? – Give an example
Gives feedback on your learning	
Increases your motivation	
Helps you work to your strengths	
Predicts future potential	
Demonstrates skills mastery	

Now share some of your examples with others in your class. Did the other students have examples you had not thought about?

Learning Point 4

One of the key purposes of any assessment is to give you feedback on your work so you can identify areas where you could improve your learning and also check your progress against your learning goals.

For formative assessment feedback gives you information on the qualities of your work and what was missing. It also gives you advice on how you could improve the work submitted so you can then implement this in your learning the next time.

For summative assessments the feedback given tends to be grades or marks indicating your level of achievement in your learning at a particular point in time.

In the next lesson you will look at two further assessment activities, self-assessment and peer assessment, where you will explore further how work may be assessed and feedback provided.

PAUSE AND REFLECT

1. What have you learned in this lesson?

_____

_____

2. How did you learn this?

_____

_____

3. How can you use what you learned in your schoolwork/study?

_____

_____

MENTAL NOTE

"It's going to be hard, but hard is not impossible." – Anon

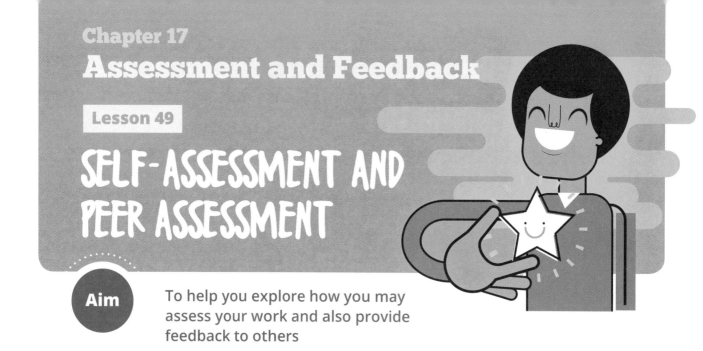

Lesson 49

SELF-ASSESSMENT AND PEER ASSESSMENT

Aim To help you explore how you may assess your work and also provide feedback to others

Learning Point 1

As you have seen, feedback is very important to help you improve the quality of your work. However, up until now, whilst you may have been reflecting on your work, you might not have been critically assessing the quality of your work. Being able to critically assess your own work helps you identify the areas of strengths within your work and possible weaker areas that need improving. If you are more aware of how your work is assessed then you will be more conscious of what you need to do to achieve higher marks.

EXERCISE 1

The Skills of Assessment

Read the following extract which a student wrote for an assessment. When you have finished reading the extract look at the marking sheet which follows and see how you would assess it.

Question: Write an introductory paragraph for a speech to the UN dealing with the challenge of obesity.

"Good afternoon, Secretary General, your excellencies, ladies and gentlemen and distinguished guests. Thank you so much for allowing me to talk to you about the damning effects of childhood and teenage obesity both in Ireland and on a global scale.

Ten to fifteen per cent of Irish people are living with diabetes. This figure is set to rise to twenty per cent by 2025; that is one-fifth of our population. I believe we can make a change if we own up to our eating habits and address the causes of the problem.

For so many years weight has been considered a taboo topic and people didn't accept that overeating was part of a medical condition that often stemmed from other issues, for example mental health.

Currently the figures are drastic, with thousands of patients crammed into diabetic wards and clinics; patients feeling isolated and neglected in their homes because they are not getting appropriate support. It is not too late but now is the time, now is going to be the difference."

Think carefully about how well you think the student did. For each assessment criteria score the following:

Red = Needs improving

Amber = Average/okay

Green = Good

Skills	Red	Amber	Green
Neat presentation *(10 marks)*			
Correct spelling *(10 marks)*			
Writing in their own words *(10 marks)*			
Did they use capital letters, full stops and commas well? *(10 marks)*			

Structure	Red	Amber	Green
The paragraph make sense as you read through it. *(20 marks)*			
Evidence is given to back up their arguments. *(20 marks)*			

Score this piece out of 100. Give a reason for your answer.	
	/100

Suggest some ways this student could improve their answer.

EXERCISE 2

Self-assessment

Now that you are more aware of what is involved in assessing a piece of work, are you ready to assess a piece of your own work?

Choose an essay that you might have completed recently – it doesn't matter what it is on – and complete the following assessment sheet for yourself.

Think carefully about how well you think you did. For each assessment criteria score the following:

Red = Needs improving

Amber = Average/okay

Green = Good

Skills	Red	Amber	Green
Neat presentation (10 marks)			
Correct spelling (10 marks)			
Written in your own words (10 marks)			
Did you use capital letters, full stops and commas well? (10 marks)			

Structure	Red	Amber	Green
The essay makes sense as you read through it. *(10 marks)*			
Introduction, middle and conclusion *(10 marks)*			
Examples given as evidence to back up any arguments *(10 marks)*			
Research is evident through examples given *(10 marks)*			

Score this piece out of 100. Give a reason for your answer.	
	/100

Suggest some ways to improve your answer.

PAUSE AND REFLECT

1. What have you learned in this lesson?

2. How did you learn this?

3. How can you use what you learned in your schoolwork/study?

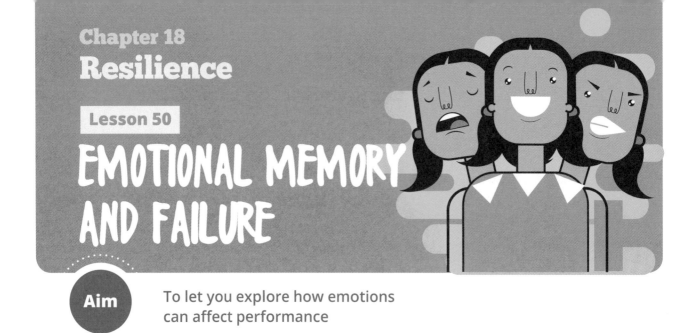

Chapter 18
Resilience

Lesson 50

EMOTIONAL MEMORY AND FAILURE

Aim To let you explore how emotions can affect performance

 Learning Point 1

In the last two lessons we discussed assessments. In this lesson you explore some of the emotions you might have around doing assessments. In lesson 35 on changing beliefs, you learned how your thoughts and emotions can affect your actions and therefore the outcomes you get. As you know, your emotions can be very powerful and so they can impact on your performance, especially when it comes to assessment time.

 EXERCISE 1

Emotions

Here is a list of feeling words describing certain emotions. Can you choose a feeling word to describe how you might feel in the following situations?

> Motivated, annoyed, angry, worried, stressed, nervous, excited, bored, peaceful, surprised, tired, confident, hyper, lazy, frustrated, confused, scared, happy

a. Doing homework?

_____

b. Taking a test?

_____

c. Reading a book for fun?

d. Reading a book for school?

e. Emailing a friend?

f. Writing an essay?

g. Presenting your work to others?

h. Going to sleep?

i. Getting up in the morning?

Look back at your answers and now answer the rest.

j. Do any of your feelings get in the way of you doing your best?
☐ Yes ☐ No

k. Which feelings get in the way?

l. Do any of your feelings aid you doing your best?   ☐ Yes ☐ No

m. Which feelings might aid you?

How are you Feeling?

People naturally have different kinds of feelings about assessments. It is important to recognise these feelings and know how they might impact you. Here is a list of emotions. Take some time to go through each of these and tick the ones that best describe how you feel about assessments. You can tick more than one.

Worried

Unhappy

Peaceful

Confused

Scared

Confident

Happy

Excited

a. Can you describe briefly why you might be feeling this way about assessment?

_____

_____

b. How do you think this might impact on your performance?

_____

_____

 Learning Point 2

Two of the most common emotions students have around assessments are being scared and being worried. You might have put a tick beside them yourself. One of the reasons students feel scared or worried is because they are afraid of failure. Nobody likes to fail at anything. However, most people don't look at failure properly.

People tend to see failure as an end point, once they fail at something that's it, nothing more can be done. However, this is not the case, instead:

> ***Failure is an event on the road to success – It is only a temporary state.***

In life, everybody fails at things in many ways. Failure must be seen as an opportunity for growth. Just think of some of these famous failures:

→ JK Rowling's manuscript for Harry Potter was turned down by 30 different publishers.

→ Bill Gates was a Harvard dropout.

→ Walt Disney was fired from a newspaper for having no imagination and no original ideas.

→ Steve Jobs, at age 30, was sacked from the company he founded.

→ Thomas Edison's teacher told him he was too stupid to learn anything at school.

→ Dr Seuss was rejected by 27 publishers.

→ Michael Jordan was cut from his high school team and went home to his room to cry.

Failure is not ideal, it is not what you have strived for but it happens and you need to learn how to deal with it. The most important part of a conversation around failure is WHAT YOU DID about it, what did you learn from the situation and how could you avoid it happening again?

EXERCISE 3

Successful Failures

Read through the list of famous people who failed in the past and answer the following questions, you might want to discuss the answers with others in your class.

a. How many of these people were remembered as failures?

_____

b. What did all of these people have in common?

_____

c. What can this teach you?

_____

 Learning Point 3

One of the key skills that is really important to learn in today's world is the ability to keep going, to try again, to bounce back after failure. This is called resilience and you will learn all about it in the coming lessons.

 PAUSE AND REFLECT

1. What have you learned in this lesson?

_____

_____

2. How did you learn this?

_____

_____

3. How can you use what you learned in your schoolwork/study?

_____

_____

Chapter 18
Resilience

Lesson 51
EMOTIONS AND RESILIENCE

Aim To explore the concept of resilience

 Learning Point 1

In the last lesson you learned that failure is an important step on the road to success. Unfortunately a lot of people give up at the first hurdle or obstacle they meet. This may be because they haven't developed resilience. If you wish to be successful in your learning journey then you too need to learn to develop resilience. It is something that is really important throughout life.

 Learning Point 2

Resilience is your ability to bounce back and continue after you have met an obstacle or set-back, like a failure in a test or low score on an essay. It is having the ability to bounce back and continue on your journey to reach your goals. BOUNCE is an acronym which teaches you about resilience:

B Bad things and times happen but things do get better.

O Others are there to help you but you need to let them know.

U Unhelpful thoughts don't make things better.

N Nobody is perfect.

C Concentrate on the good things in your life, it's not all bad.

E Everybody has setbacks or struggles. You are not on your own here.

During this lesson you will explore five ways you can build your resilience. These are:

Express yourself Nourish yourself  Sunny side up  Identify your strenghts Relax

Learning Point 3

Express yourself: Don't bottle things up, ***express your emotions***. You explored earlier how powerful they are. Along with having people who you can talk things through with, you could also express your emotions by keeping a diary, through painting, or even music.

Everybody Needs Somebody

It is important to know who you have around you that you can talk to about things. In the diagram below fill in each circle with the various people in your life.

a. In the centre circle write the names of those in your life with whom you can discuss anything.

b. In the next circle are people in your life who you can go to for advice.

c. In the outer circle write the names of agencies or support services available to you if you needed them.

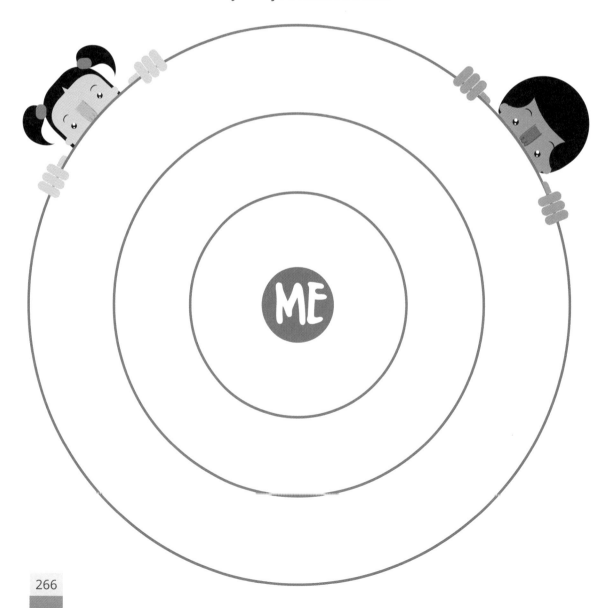

Learning Point 4

Nourish yourself: The Romans used to have a saying about a healthy mind in a healthy body. To be effective in your learning and to feel positive means living a healthy, balanced life, getting the required amount of sleep, eating properly and exercising. There is a further lesson to look at these.

Healthy mind IN A healthy body

 ## Learning Point 5

Sunny side up: In lesson 34 you looked at beliefs and self-beliefs. When people meet obstacles on their journey, negative thinking can creep in.

It is important to check your thinking to see whether you are thinking negative or positive thoughts. Positive thinking will give you the **motivation to keep going**.

EXERCISE 2

Attitude of Gratitude

One easy way of changing your negative thinking into positive thinking is by developing what is called an attitude of gratitude. This simply means reminding yourself of the good things in your life. What's going well for you? What are you grateful for?

Check in with yourself to see how positive you are about your life. In the box that follows write in 20 things that you are grateful for here and now.

(i)	(xi)
(ii)	(xii)
(iii)	(xiii)
(iv)	(xiv)
(v)	(xv)
(vi)	(xvi)
(vii)	(xvii)
(viii)	(xviii)
(ix)	(xix)
(x)	(xx)

a. Did you find it easy to write in 20 things?

☐ **Yes** ☐ **No**

Explain:

_____

_____

_____

⚙ Learning Point 6

Identify your strengths: Everybody has their own particular set of strengths. By working to your strengths you will experience success. You build your confidence by experiencing success so when things go wrong you will have the confidence to pick up and try again.

EXERCISE 3 Your Strengths

Can you remember your learning strengths, which you identified in Section 2? Fill in your top 3 below.

1. _____

2. _____

3. _____

⚙ Learning Point 7

Relax: It is important to take time out, to relax and unwind. Focusing all the time on your learning and studying is not good for you. It is important that you take regular breaks from your study and you have a variety of ways of switching off or winding down, which is what relaxing is about. One powerful relaxation tool is **mindfulness**. This is a technique of bringing your attention to the present by focusing on what is around you and not letting it wander off worrying about other things. It might be something that you could investigate further and learn more about. In today's hectic world more and more people are turning to mindfulness exercises.

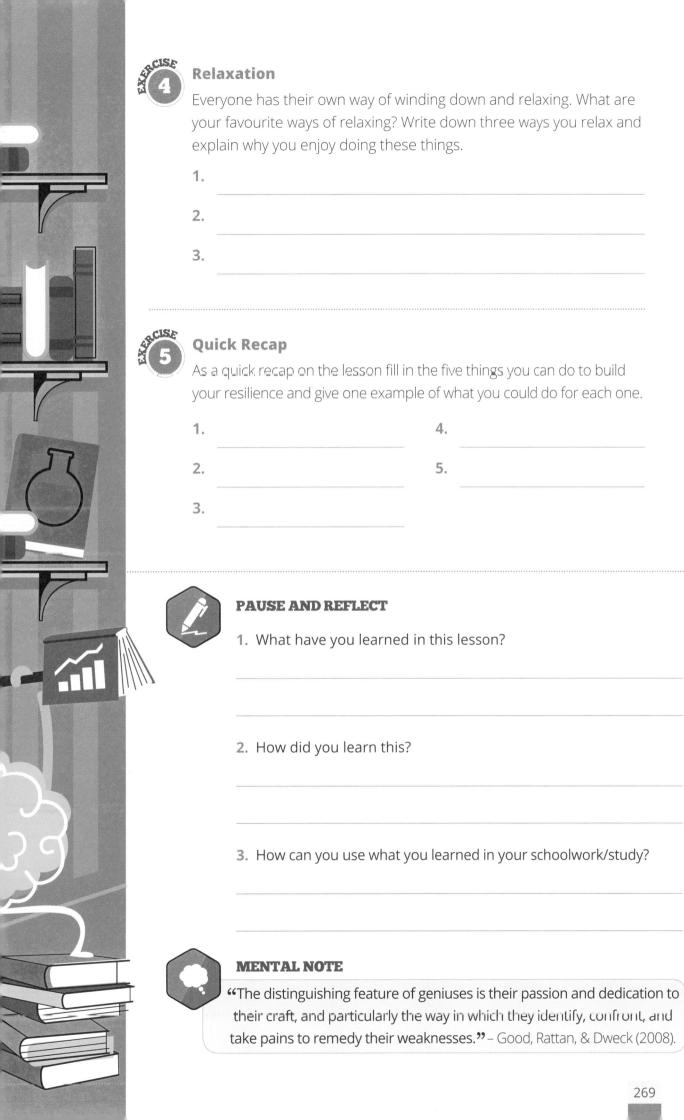

EXERCISE 4

Relaxation

Everyone has their own way of winding down and relaxing. What are your favourite ways of relaxing? Write down three ways you relax and explain why you enjoy doing these things.

1. _____

2. _____

3. _____

EXERCISE 5

Quick Recap

As a quick recap on the lesson fill in the five things you can do to build your resilience and give one example of what you could do for each one.

1. _____   4. _____

2. _____   5. _____

3. _____

PAUSE AND REFLECT

1. What have you learned in this lesson?

_____

_____

2. How did you learn this?

_____

_____

3. How can you use what you learned in your schoolwork/study?

_____

_____

MENTAL NOTE

"The distinguishing feature of geniuses is their passion and dedication to their craft, and particularly the way in which they identify, confront, and take pains to remedy their weaknesses." – Good, Rattan, & Dweck (2008).

Lesson 52

GROWTH MINDSET

Aim To explore the concepts of growth and fixed mindsets

 **Learning Point 1**

Most people who are resilient also have what is called a **growth mindset**. Some people believe they are born with a limit to their intelligence and ability. However, you should know by now that this is not true. Most people have multiple intelligences which they use and grow by having goals and focus and by putting them into action so that they can succeed.

This is what is called having a growth mindset. Mindset is about the attitude or approach that people take to success, especially when it comes to their learning. The two types are growth and fixed mindset. Here is an explanation of both:

What kind of mindset do you have?

I can learn anything I want to.
When I'm frustrated, I persevere.
I want to challenge myself.
When I fail, I learn.
Tell me I try hard.
If you succeed, I'm inspired.
My efforts and attitude determine everything.

I'm either good at it, or I'm not.
When I'm frustrated, I give up.
I don't like to be challenged.
When I fail, I'm no good.
Tell me I'm smart.
If you succeed, I feel threatened.
My abilities determine everything.

EXERCISE 1

Which Mindset do you Have?

This exercise will help you determine the type of mindset you are inclined to have. Read through the following statements and indicate to what extent you would agree or disagree.

a. You have a certain amount of intelligence, and you can't really do much to change it.

(Agree)   (Maybe)   (Disagree)

b. No matter who you are, you can significantly change your intelligence level.

(Agree)   (Maybe)   (Disagree)

c. You can learn new things but you can't change your underlying level of intelligence.

(Agree)   (Maybe)   (Disagree)

d. Learning new things can increase your underlying intelligence.

(Agree)   (Maybe)   (Disagree)

e. Talent is something you're born with, not something you can develop.

(Agree)   (Maybe)   (Disagree)

f. If you practise something for long enough, you can develop a talent for it.

(Agree)   (Maybe)   (Disagree)

g. People who are good at a particular skill were born with a higher level of natural ability.

(Agree)   (Maybe)   (Disagree)

h. People who are good at a particular skill have spent a lot of time practising that skill, regardless of natural ability.

(Agree)   (Maybe)   (Disagree)

i. You can always substantially change how much talent you have.

(Agree)   (Maybe)   (Disagree)

j. You can learn new things, but you can't really change your basic level of talent.

(Agree)   (Maybe)   (Disagree)

Now work out your score:

Step 1: Check which statements are growth mindset or fixed mindset statements and write either F or G beside each one.

① = Fixed **②** = Growth **③** = Fixed **④** = Growth **⑤** = Fixed

⑥ = Growth **⑦** = Fixed **⑧** = Growth **⑨** = Growth **⑩** = Fixed

Step 2: For growth statements give yourself the following scores:

④ = Agree **②** = Maybe **⓪** = Disagree

For fixed statements give yourself the following scores:

⓪ = Agree **②** = Maybe **④** = Disagree

Then add up your total score for the exercise.

Step 3: Your results

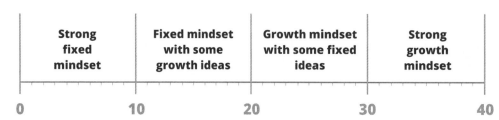

| | Strong fixed mindset | Fixed mindset with some growth ideas | Growth mindset with some fixed ideas | Strong growth mindset | |

0   10   20   30   40

a. So what mindset do you have? _____

b. Are you surprised? ☐ Yes ☐ No

c. Why? _____

Developing and nurturing a growth mindset towards life and learning can provide you with positive outcomes.

Learning Point 2

Success is not all about attitude but also about effort and strategy. Einstein once said that if you keep doing the same thing in the same way you will keep on getting the same results. So if you are doing something wrong no matter how hard you try you will still end up getting it wrong. A key element of having a growth mindset is the ability to reflect on what you are doing and if it is not working to readjust and try doing it a different way. You are not giving up, you are simply taking a different approach or strategy.

Mindset Strategies

For the following situations, using a growth mindset can you think of strategies for improving the situation?

a. You put a lot of effort into passing an assessment yet you failed.

    _____

    _____

b. You practise a lot as a basketball team yet you keep losing games.

    _____

    _____

c. You get stuck on a maths problem and feel you are no good at maths.

    _____

    _____

d. You are not putting any effort into class yet you are still passing.

    _____

    _____

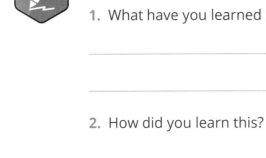

PAUSE AND REFLECT

1. What have you learned in this lesson?

    _____

    _____

2. How did you learn this?

    _____

    _____

3. How can you use what you learned in your schoolwork/study?

    _____

    _____

Coping with Stress

Lesson 53

WHAT IS STRESS?

Aim To learn about stress and how it can affect you

 Learning Point 1

At times everyone experiences stress, especially when assignments are due or exams are near. So what is stress? Stress is your body's way of responding to demands placed upon you. When you feel stressed your body releases chemicals into your blood. These chemicals give you more energy and strength, which can be a good thing if you are in danger or participating in a competition. However, if this stress is a response to something emotional and there is no outlet for the extra energy and strength this can be detrimental to your health.

Stress is a word that is casually used in everyday conversation, often in a negative way. It is often misunderstood. **You NEED some stress to keep motivated, to drive you to succeed and move onwards.** However, when stress gets to the stage where it impacts your normal ability to function then there is a problem.

What causes you to feel stress?

Stress is your body's response to situations you feel you do not have the resources to deal with.

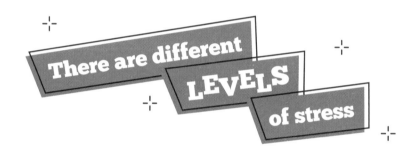

There are different LEVELS of stress

You might be anxious and excited before an important football match or you might be anxious and worried about how you will do in school.

Stress can be short term or can last for longer periods, maybe over days or weeks. When stress lasts for longer periods of time it really affects us in a negative way.

When you see something as a threat, the body triggers a 'fight or flight' response mode. You feel stress and prepare to tackle the threat. This is a natural response for many mammals, including humans. We must all decide which option to take, 'fight' the threat or 'flight' i.e. run away!

Common Stress Factors

Here is a list of common stress factors for young people. Tick the ones that cause you stress, you can add to this list if there are other things causing you stress that are not mentioned here.

a. Homework

b. Exams

c. Sports competitions

d. Trouble with a teacher

e. Falling out with a friend

f. Arguments with siblings

g. Trouble with parent/guardian

h. Feeling left out

i. Being bullied or teased

j. Learning subjects you don't like

k. Trying to make new friends

l. Feeling like you don't fit in

m. Missing one of your parents

n. Other ......

Stress in the Body

On the body map draw in the places where you think people might usually feel or experience stress. In the thought bubble write down any thoughts you can think of that can cause stress at times, especially self-talk around the time of exams.

 **Learning Point 2**

Stress can negatively impact you if not recognised or managed properly. Here are some of the ways it can have an impact:

→ **Affects performance** – impacts your ability to think, make smart decisions and have fun.

→ **Affects your health** – it can cause pain or stiffness in shoulders and back, cause headaches and stomach aches along with other discomforts.

→ **Affects relationships** – you might get irritable and say things you might later regret, impacts on your relationship with siblings, parents, teachers and friends.

 Check your Stress

Now that you are more aware of where stress may be found in the body, are you aware of how you might feel it in your body? Complete this short checklist.

Place a tick next to any of the symptoms of stress you might experience at times.

○ **a.** Difficulty sleeping   ○ **i.** Shortness of breath

○ **b.** Tight chest   ○ **j.** Lack of concentration

○ **c.** Racing/pounding heart   ○ **k.** Stiff neck and/or shoulders

○ **d.** Headaches   ○ **l.** Upset stomach

○ **e.** Poor appetite   ○ **m.** Feeling out of control

○ **f.** Depression   ○ **n.** Argumentative

○ **g.** Unclear thinking   ○ **o.** Other ......

○ **h.** Poor memory

Learning Point 3

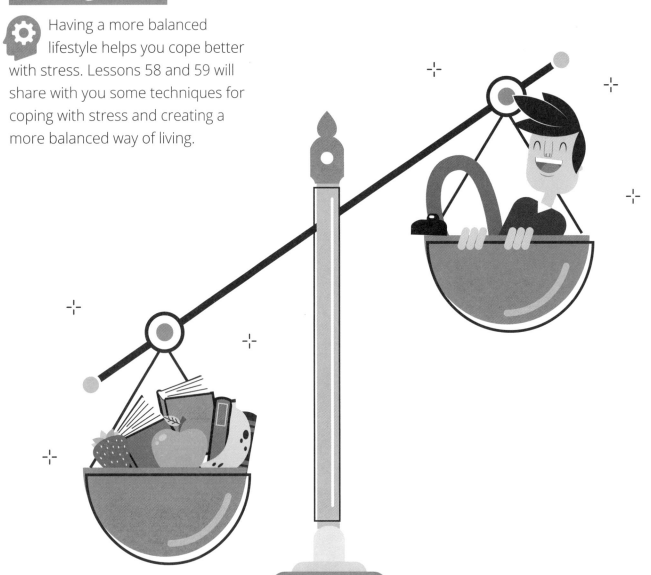

Having a more balanced lifestyle helps you cope better with stress. Lessons 58 and 59 will share with you some techniques for coping with stress and creating a more balanced way of living.

PAUSE AND REFLECT

1. What have you learned in this lesson?

_____

_____

2. How did you learn this?

_____

_____

3. How can you use what you learned in your schoolwork/study?

_____

_____

Chapter 19
Coping with Stress

Lesson 54

COPING WITH STRESS

Aim　To learn about stress and how it can affect you

 ## Learning Point 1

It is important to remember what you learned in the last lesson, that nobody makes you stressed out, it is simply the way that you feel about what is happening that determines whether or not you are stressed out. As you know, feelings are very powerful, so this lesson will explore with you some simple strategies that you can use to help you control your reactions to things happening around you. If you can control your reactions to the little things that aren't worth getting upset about, then you will be more able to keep your stress levels down when there's a crisis or something more challenging happening in your life.

 EXERCISE 1

Responding to Stress

This short survey will help you identify the different ways that you respond to stress. People tend to respond to stress in three different ways, which are:

React and blame

Run and hide

Cope positively

Here is a quick survey for you, try to be as honest as possible.
Tick the responses that you normally have when stressed.

1. React and Blame		2. Run and Hide		3. Cope Positively	
Feel sorry for yourself	◯	Eat junk food	◯	Talk to your parents	◯
Complain	◯	Watch loads of TV	◯	Talk to your friends	◯
Break things	◯	Spend loads of time on social media	◯	Talk to a teacher	◯
Lash out at others	◯	Just bury it	◯	Go for a walk	◯
Get anxious and nervous	◯	Avoid people and/or situations	◯	Play with your pet	◯
Get angry	◯	Give up and stop trying	◯	Do your favourite thing	◯
Become easily irritated	◯	Lose yourself in your music	◯	Listen to relaxing music	◯
Pick a fight	◯	Stick to yourself	◯	Work out	◯
Blame others	◯	Sleep a lot	◯	Other....	◯
Other....	◯	Other....	◯	Other....	◯

a. Depending on the situation, people tend to try a variety
of options. Which response was your most dominant?

_____

_____

b. What does this tell you?

_____

Learning Point 2

This is how these various responses really impact on you:

i. **When you react and blame** – When you are letting off emotional steam
like this, you are probably adding more stress to your body and you could
even make the situation worse by lashing out at others.

ii. **When you try to run and hide** – This is only an avoidance strategy and
the reality is the stress is still there, all you did was bury it, and sometimes
someone else will trigger something in you, causing an even greater explosion.

iii. **When you try to cope positively** – These strategies can be relaxing and soothing for a while, however the stress can keep coming back.

So what do you do? Well the first thing is to give yourself a chance to change perspective so you can respond rather than react. **Perspective** is really important because it determines how we see the world around us and therefore how we act. This simple illustration by Ebbinghaus (the same guy who came up with the forgetting curve) shows us how important perspective is. Would you believe that both orange circles are the same size?

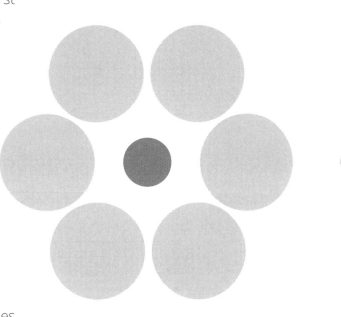

 Learning Point 3

Redirecting your focus can be helpful in stressful times because it helps you change the perspective you might have on a situation. Here is an example of 'redirecting focus.'

Example: You need to take a penalty kick

I hate the pressure of taking a penalty kick in a football game.

I like the challenge of conquering my nerves, calming my fears and visualising the ball sail over the bar.

(i) The challenge response brings out your **BEST** qualities.

(ii) The pressure response brings out your **WORST** fears.

EXERCISE 2

Challenge vs Pressure Statements!

Complete the following statements:

a. I hate the pressure of

   _____

   I like the challenge of

   _____

b. I hate the pressure of

   _____

   I like the challenge of

   _____

c. I hate the pressure of

   _____

   I like the challenge of

   _____

 Learning Point 4

As stated previously, stress is caused by how you perceive something and then react, so the key is to give yourself the opportunity to respond rather than react.

Here are some simple steps that will help you.

(i) **Pause** – Recognise that you are feeling stressed. Halt whatever it is you're doing so you can put your thoughts and emotions on hold. Pay attention to your breathing. This simple action of checking your breathing and trying to slow it down will help stop your thoughts and feelings from running away with you and bring some clarity to the situation.

(ii) **Pose the question** – Ask yourself if there is a better way to handle the situation that would reduce the stress. If you get stuck try and activate a positive feeling, positive feelings help you see more clearly.

(iii) **Check in** – Notice if there is any change in the way you think or feel about the situation now.

Pause   **Pose the question**   **Check in**

EXERCISE 3

Strategy for Dealing with Stress

Check now to see if you're feeling stressed about anything. If not, then think of a time recently when you were stressed out. Now apply the steps to see what happens!

a. Pause – What is the situation?

_____

b. Pose the question if there is a better way to handle this — what would you do?

_____

_____

c. Check in to see if anything has changed in how you think and feel.

_____

_____

EXERCISE 4

Coping with Assessments

Try to check in with yourself about how you truly feel about assessments and exams. Try the various steps again

a. Pause – What is the situation?

_____

b. Pose the question if there is a better way to handle this — what would you do?

_____

c. Check in to see if anything has changed in how you think and feel.

_____

If you get stressed during an exam, how do you think you could use the steps?

a. Pause – What is the situation?

_____

b. Pose the question if there is a better way to handle this — what would you do?

_____

c. Check in to see if anything has changed in how you think and feel.

_____

Learning Point 5

These steps can help you in assignments by:

(i) Creating clarity and defogging the brain

(ii) Putting feelings of anxiety on hold

(iii) Increasing focus

(iv) Getting you through sticky situations

(v) Helping you recover from difficult questions/ papers

(vi) Avoiding careless mistakes

(vii) Neutralising feelings of frustration.

 PAUSE AND REFLECT

1. What have you learned in this lesson?

_____

_____

2. How did you learn this?

_____

_____

3. How can you use what you learned in your schoolwork/study?

_____

_____

 MENTAL NOTE

"All our dreams can come true – if we have the courage to pursue them." – Walt Disney

Chapter 19
Coping with Stress

Lesson 55
A BALANCED, HEALTHY YOU

Aim To look at how important balance is in life in order to achieve

Learning Point 1

Previously you learned about how important a healthy diet, sleep, exercise and a good routine are to helping reduce your stress and succeed in your learning. This is called having a balanced lifestyle. Your physical health directly affects your mental health, so to remain healthy you need to ensure that you are eating the right things, getting enough sleep and exercising regularly. More than ever you need this balance in your life around the time of assessments or exams.

EXERCISE 1

Survey of Habits

This survey will help you to create an overview of how balanced your lifestyle currently is and identify if any changes may be needed.

Eating and drinking

a. How many glasses of water do you normally drink a day?

b. How many should you drink?

c. What do you normally eat for breakfast?

_____

_____

d. Would this breakfast give you enough energy if you were
doing an assessment today? ☐ Yes ☐ No

e. What kind of snacks do you normally eat?

_____

f. What types of snacks should you eat?

_____

_____

Sleep

g. How many hours of sleep did you get last night? ☐

h. How many hours of sleep do you normally get? ☐

i. Do you turn off your phone, iPad etc.
before going to bed? ☐ Yes ☐ No

j. If not, do you bring them to bed with you? ☐ Yes ☐ No

Exercise

k. Do you regularly exercise each day? ☐ Yes ☐ No

l. If you should be exercising at least 30 minutes each day, what
extra would you need to do to achieve this?

_____

m. Do you think it is important to keep this up during assessment time?

_____

n. Why?

_____

_____

Study

o. Do you have a regular routine for your
homework and study? ☐ Yes ☐ No

p. Do you stick to this routine? ☐ Yes ☐ No

q. Have you got your study planned out? ☐ Yes ☐ No

r. Do you put your homework and study
off until the last minute? ☐ Yes ☐ No

Stress and negative emotions

s. Do you get stressed before a big exam?

Yes   Sometimes   No

t. When you get anxious about your exam do you tend to dwell on it?

Yes   Sometimes   No

u. Do you regularly hear yourself repeating negative self-talk?

Yes   Sometimes   No

v. Do you try to change this negative self-talk to positive thinking?

Yes   Sometimes   No

w. When you are stressed do you talk to others about it?

Yes   Sometimes   No

⚙ Learning Point 2

Here are some tips to help guide you in achieving a more balanced lifestyle.

Eating and drinking: Your body in some ways is like an engine and needs the right fuel to operate effectively. You need to eat properly to ensure you have the right amount of nutrition to help keep you going when you are studying and especially around assessment time. A good diet consists of a mixture of the following:

i. Eating complex carbohydrates like wholegrain breads, brown pasta, raspberries, sweet potatoes will give you a slow release of energy over a number of hours along with helping you feel more relaxed and less stressed.

ii. Healthy fats like omega 3 from fish oil tablets or from fresh fish help the brain function better.

iii. Proteins are an essential brain food and help keep you alert during assessments. Eggs, dairy products, whole grains, green leafy vegetables are good sources of protein.

iv. Good sources of vitamins are leafy vegetables, cranberries, bananas, nuts and seeds.

v. Avoid high energy drinks and caffeine as these will only give you short bursts of energy and leave you drained.

287

Sleep: Sleep is really important for learning. When you go to sleep at night everything you have learned during the day is transferred to your long-term memory. Aim to sleep for 8 hours a day. Less or even more than this can tire you out. Try and avoid sitting up late cramming around exam times. Remember, your brain needs this sleep time to process the learning.

Exercise: Do something energetic each day, walking, swimming, running etc. This gets rid of pent-up energy or anxiety along with getting some fresh oxygen into your brain, which helps you learn. You should aim for at least 30 minutes around exam time.

Study: Remember your study timetable in your study journal at the end of this book. Stick to your timetable and give yourself regular breaks.

Managing negative emotions: If you find yourself feeling stressed then remind yourself of the five simple things you can do that help you be more resilient:

Coping Plan

Following on from the last exercise, can you identify some goals that you can set yourself that will help you cope better around exam time?

a. Healthy eating goals _____

b. Sleep goals _____

c. Exercise goals _____

d. Study goals _____

e. Stress and negative emotions goals _____

If you can work on achieving these goals then you will be well on the way to achieving a balanced lifestyle that will greatly help you in managing, coping and succeeding in your assessments and other stressful periods in your life.

Reduce the Stress

Here are some common student comments around the time of assessments or exams when they are feeling under pressure. Can you consider some possible solutions or advice that you could give that would help in these situations?

a. The last month is the worst. The pressure just keeps building up and I don't know how to cope with all the work.

Possible solution

_____

_____

b. I've got three weeks of exams and I don't know how I am going to get through them.

Possible solution

c. During the last few weeks, I've been really miserable, I've been doing nothing but work as I have so much to do to get ready.

Possible solution

d. I only feel guilty when I take a break so I just keep at it.

Possible solution

e. I need coffee and plenty of comfort food to keep me going as I find myself working to all hours each night.

Possible solution

PAUSE AND REFLECT

1. What have you learned in this lesson?

2. How did you learn this?

3. How can you use what you learned in your schoolwork/study?

MENTAL NOTE

"There are no shortcuts to any place worth going." – Helen Keller

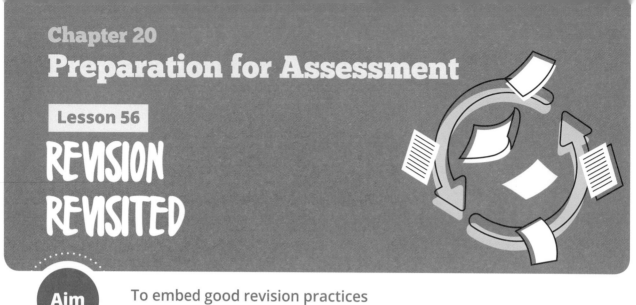

Preparation for Assessment

Lesson 56

REVISION REVISITED

Aim To embed good revision practices for assessments

 Learning Point 1

In the last few lessons you have been learning how to cope with stress, especially when assessments are involved. When you were looking at revision in the last section you learned that revision helps ease a lot of the stress and pressure associated with assessments because you feel more confident about what you know.

Revision is not simply about memorising but rather it is a way of pulling together and putting structure on everything you have learned.

Quick Check in on Revision Progress

Hopefully at this stage you have begun to use your study journal at the end of this workbook to help you with your revision. Here is a quick checklist to review how you are getting on. For each question circle the most appropriate response.

a. Have you created your study timetable?

(Not yet) (Somewhat) (All complete)

b. Have you organised your study area?

(Not yet) (Somewhat) (All complete)

c. Have you broken down your subjects into the various topics?

(Not yet) (Somewhat) (All complete)

d. Have you filled in your study journal with all your subjects and topics?

(Not yet) (Somewhat) (All complete)

e. Have you created your one-page summaries for each topic?

(Not yet) (Somewhat) (All complete)

f. Have you been recording your **5 x 5 Review** in your study journal?

(Not yet) (Somewhat) (All complete)

g. How do you think you are progressing with your revision overall? Give reasons for answers.

_____

_____

_____

Learning Point 2

The Power of Habit: Charles Duhig wrote a book called the 'Power of Habit', where he talks about how 80% of our success is determined not by how intelligent or smart or talented we are – but by our habits. So success in our revision is determined by us getting into the habit of revision.

Good habits lead to improved motivation. Once in a good routine, you should stick to it, reward yourself, and you will set yourself up to repeat this pattern. Plan your revision using your study journal and stick to it. Decide on how you are going to reward yourself for sticking to your routine i.e. by giving yourself small breaks, allowing yourself extra time on social media, etc. This will motivate you or cue you up to continue on with your revision. Most people struggle with revision because they don't make a habit of it.

This diagram helps you remember how the power of habit works.

The more routine and resulting rewards you build into your life, the more motivated you become as you begin to see results over time. It is VERY important to be patient, habits don't happen overnight!

....

What Needs Changing?

Having reviewed your progress in revision in the previous exercise, what three things could you do to help you get into the habit of regular revision?

a. 1. _____

    2. _____

    3. _____

> Give this some thought, there is no point writing something down if you are not going to do it.

292

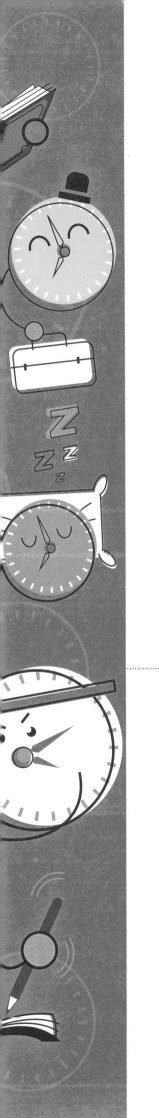

b. What would prevent you from putting these into practice?

_____

_____

c. How could you overcome these challenges?

_____

_____

d. Do you need support from anybody? Who?

_____

_____

You may wish to share your answers with other people in your class. Sometimes others' encouragement and support can help keep you focused and on task.

PAUSE AND REFLECT

1. What have you learned in this lesson?

_____

_____

2. How did you learn this?

_____

_____

3. How can you use what you learned in your schoolwork/study?

_____

_____

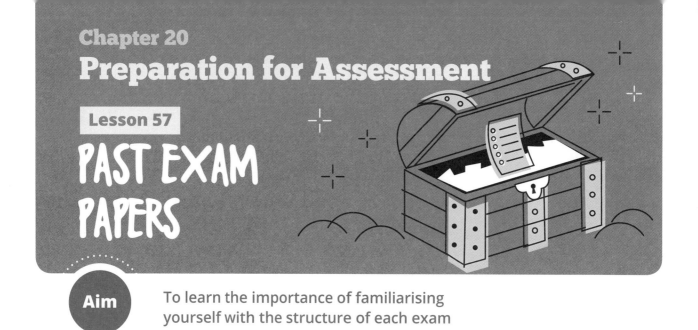

Lesson 57
PAST EXAM PAPERS

Aim To learn the importance of familiarising yourself with the structure of each exam

 ## Learning Point 1

In Section 2 you learned how to create your own notes for studying called one-page summaries and hopefully went on to create these as mind maps. By Christmas term of third year you should now have a folder with all your one-page summaries for each subject which you are using for your **5 x 5 Review**. In this lesson you will learn how to use other study aids which can help you when revising and preparing for exams.

 ## Learning Point 2

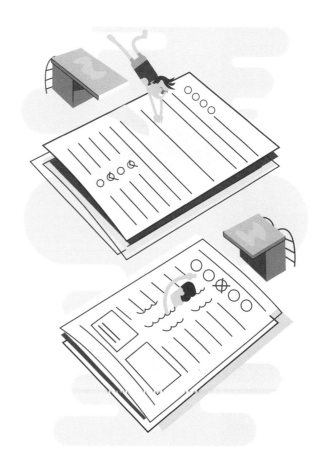

Past exam papers are a valuable resource for you when revising. By going over past exam papers you are familiarising yourself with the structure and layout of the paper for each subject.

It is important that you have familiarised yourself with the layout of each paper for each exam, so that you are not wasting time during the exam on what might be coming up next. Using your past exam papers you can create an exam checklist for yourself for each exam. You can then take these out the day before to briefly remind yourself of what to expect.

EXERCISE 1

Exam Layout

Using your past exam papers for Science, complete this exam checklist template. Read through the layout of the exam paper closely before you begin.

Subject:

Total marks available for this paper:

Length of time of paper:

How many sections are there to the paper?

Section_____   _____Questions

Section_____   _____Questions

Section_____   _____Questions

How many questions must be answered?

Are there compulsory questions? ☐ Yes ☐ No

Which ones?

What questions are optional?

How many marks are allocated for each long answer question?

Based on marks, how much time needs to be spent on each question?

Question _____   Marks _____   Time _____

Question _____   Marks _____   Time _____

Question _____   Marks _____   Time _____

Question _____   Marks _____   Time _____

Question _____   Marks _____   Time _____

Question _____   Marks _____   Time _____

Time allowed for reading through and choosing questions?

Time allowed for checking over answers?

Any unusual features of this paper? ☐ Yes ☐ No

What are they?

Which aids – dictionaries, calculators, etc. – are allowed in this exam?

Do you need to bring in any other equipment? (e.g. colouring pencils) ☐ Yes ☐ No

What?

Now create an exam checklist template for each subject you have.

PAUSE AND REFLECT

1. What have you learned in this lesson?

_____

_____

2. How did you learn this?

_____

_____

3. How can you use what you learned in your schoolwork/study?

_____

_____

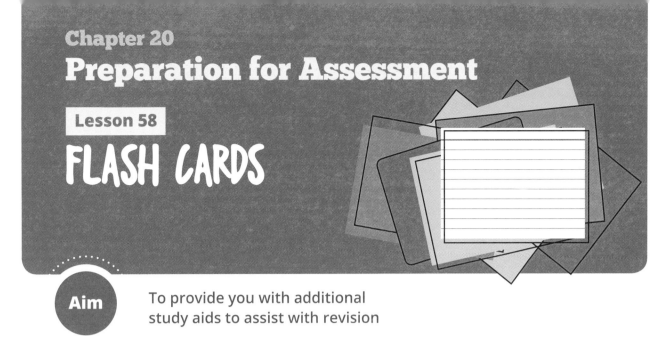

Chapter 20
Preparation for Assessment

Lesson 58
FLASH CARDS

Aim To provide you with additional study aids to assist with revision

 Learning Point 1

In Section 2 you learned how to create mind maps as one-page summaries of your various topics. Your mind map notes can be complemented by using other aids such as your past papers and flash cards to help you prepare for your assessment.

 Learning Point 2

Along with reviewing and recalling your notes it's important to practise writing answers for questions that come up in exam papers. This is a valuable use of your past exam papers.

When you go through each exam question in the past papers ask yourself the following:

→ What is the question getting at? (Underline command words and key words)

→ Which topics on the subject course does the subject relate to?

→ What themes, examples, evidence, ideas can you include in your answer?

→ What would be a good order in which to make the points?

When revising you do not need to write out a full answer every time, though it is important that you practise writing out full answers from time to time. You can use **flash cards** to help you create summary sample answers which you can file away and then take out again and again to read over.

Flash cards are a set of cards with information for a particular topic. The cards are very useful to quickly revise before exams, allowing you to revise the main points of a question belonging to a topic in a short space of time. Flash cards are easy to store and carry around. You and a friend could get together and test each other.

You can create a set of cards for questions in each topic. You could read three or four cards every night as part of your revision.

How to make flashcards:

➔ Strong light card is best to use because you will handle them many times throughout the year. They should be around the size of a normal index card (6 inches x 4 inches).

➔ Take out your exam paper and choose the question you wish to answer.

➔ On one side of the card write down the topic, then the question and the year of the question.

➔ On the other side you can write your answer using bullet points and key notes.

Here is an example of one, going back to your example used previously on the Reformation.

Reformation;

Q. Give two reasons why people thought the catholic church was in need of reform around 1500

Past papers 2017

* Abuses in the church   Ignorant priests, wealthy bishops, unworthy popes   Sixtus IV, Alexander VI had mistresses and children
* The Renaissance   people began to think for themselves - began to criticise faults within church, popes spending large amounts of money on art
* Printing press - Bible translated into German, people's ideas like Luther or Erasmus could be circulated

EXERCISE 1

A Sample Flash Card

Create a sample flash card for the following Science question:

a. Describe the composition of blood and clearly explain the role of each part of blood.

EXERCISE 2 **Create Your Own.**
You can now go and create your own flash cards by choosing topics of your choice and looking up questions on past exam papers.

PAUSE AND REFLECT

1. What have you learned in this lesson?

_____

_____

2. How did you learn this?

_____

_____

3. How can you use what you learned in your schoolwork/study?

_____

_____

Chapter 20
Preparation for Assessment

Lesson 59

FINAL PREPARATION AND THE EXAM

Aim To help you prepare for the exam itself

 Learning Point 1

This is where you get the chance to shine and show all you have learned. The key thing for you to remember here is that worrying about things that are outside of your control will only lead to more stress, so simply focus on what it is you can control.

 Being in Control

Okay, let's look at what you **do and don't** have control over so you know where to place your energy and focus. Here is a list of factors that you might or might not have control over. Read through the list and for each one decide whether or not you have control. Simply write **C** or **NC** after each one.

a. The questions that will come up on the exam paper

b. Your own preparedness for the exam

c. Your friends and/or classmates and how they are before the exam

d. Getting enough rest

e. Eating properly before and during the exam period

f. Worrying about what you wrote after the exam.

EXERCISE 2

Taking Back That Control

Now, for each one that you said you had no control over, suggest ways in which you can take this control over for yourself.

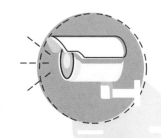

a.

_____

_____

b.

_____

_____

c.

_____

_____

d.

_____

_____

e.

_____

_____

Learning Point 2

You learned in the very first section how important having a plan and a checklist are to help you reduce stress. Simply having a structure for what you are supposed to be doing can help alleviate some of the stress. Also, when you get stressed you might end up forgetting some things so it is really important that you have a checklist prepared which you can tick off to make sure you have everything ready for the next day.

EXERCISE 3

Pre-exam Plan

Imagine that you have an exam coming up in a few weeks' time and you need to create a plan for what you will need to do the day before. Here are some prompts that will help you:

a. Include how much time you will spend at each activity.

b. Will you spend the whole day studying? If not, what else could you be doing?

Other things I need to consider to prepare myself:

Day Before

Time	Activity

c. When you're studying will you take out your notes or textbooks?_____

d. Do you spend your time cramming or familiarising yourself with the layout and structure of the exam paper? _____

e. Will you sit up late the night before cramming?_____

f. What type of food will you be eating? _____

Any other information

Learning Point 3

After all the hard work you have put into your learning and study, the last thing you will want is to not perform well in the exam. As with most things you have learned during this course, the key is in being prepared and having a system.

> *Now is the time to let yourself shine.*

EXERCISE 4

Exam Strategy Checklist

Here is a quick self-evaluation of what you might normally do when sitting an exam. Read through the questions and try to answer as honestly as possible. If you answer No, give a brief reason why that is the case.

Do you.......	Yes	No	Possible Reason
Feel confident about what you are expected to do?			
Read through the whole paper first?			
Choose the questions that you are going to do?			
Re-read the questions you have chosen before writing?			
Highlight the instruction word in the question?			
Know what time you have for each question?			
Stick to the allotted time for each question?			
Keep strictly to answering the question asked?			
Start with the easy questions and then the more difficult?			
Look around to see what others are doing?			
Give yourself time at the end to read over your answers to check for mistakes?			

b. How many No's did you have? _____

c. Did you notice anything in the responses you gave for possible reasons?   ☐ **Yes** ☐ **No**

d. What was it? _____

e. So what can you do differently in the future?

_____

_____

_____

Your Exam Strategy

Taking from what you learnt in the last exercise, write out the advice in bullet points that you would give yourself when you go into an exam.

 Learning Point 4

Here are some tips for the night before and the day of the exam:

➔ Before you finish your study check that you have everything you need ready for the following morning, exam number, pens, etc.

➔ Don't sit up cramming, make sure you get a good night's sleep.

➔ Eat well before the exam to keep up your stamina.

➔ Give yourself plenty of time to make sure you arrive on time

➔ When you get to school avoid conversations with others about what they have revised, it might only increase your stress.

➔ Once in the exam remember what you put into your exam strategy.

Learning Point 5

Your last learning point

Once your exam is over, forget about it. You have done your best and you can't do anymore so don't waste time thinking about it. The key thing is to keep your perspective, it was only an exam, only a snapshot of your learning at a particular point in time. It does not define you.

Remember all you have learned during this course, remember your strengths, and build on them. With the right attitude you can be whoever you want to be.

Learning is a lifelong journey and hopefully you have learned and developed new skills which will help you along the way.

Best of luck!

LEARNING IS A LIFELONG JOURNEY

PAUSE AND REFLECT

1. What have you learned in this lesson?

_____

_____

2. How did you learn this?

_____

_____

3. How can you use what you learned in your schoolwork/study?

_____

_____

END OF SECTION REFLECTION

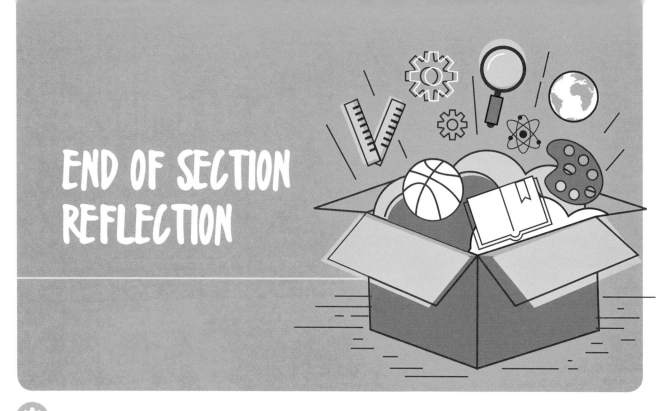

Well done, you have now completed the Learning to Learn programme! Now that you have completed the third and final section of this programme, let's pause and reflect on all that you have learned. In this part you will look at:

→ Reflecting on the Junior Cycle key skills which you developed

→ Exploring what you enjoyed most or least and why

→ Identifying how you used what you learned in other areas of your studies

→ Identifying possible areas you would like to focus on in the future.

Use the table below to rate your learning and performance from this section. Remember when considering your answers to reflect on all the variety of activities you engaged in during this section.

Managing Myself

1 Poor   **2** Fair   **3** Good   **4** Very Good   **5** Excellent

Key Skills		Student rating	Briefly Explain
Knowing myself			
I can ...	Recognise my personal strengths and weaknesses		
	Identify influences that make me who I am		
	Express my opinion		
Making considered decisions			
I can ...	Consider different options and ideas		
	Make plans and organise my work		
	Explain my choices to others		
Setting and achieving personal goals			
I can ...	Set personal goals		
	Identify what I need in order to achieve my goals		
	Ask for help when needed		
	Prepare detailed plans		
	Learn from my past actions and make changes if necessary		
Being able to reflect on my learning			
I can ...	Evaluate and reflect on my learning		
	Give and receive feedback on my learning		
	Assess my own learning and suggest ways that I can improve		

Staying Well

1 Poor   **2** Fair   **3** Good   **4** Very Good   **5** Excellent

Key Skills		Student rating	Briefly Explain
Being confident			
I can ...	Communicate my opinions and beliefs with confidence in a variety of ways		
	Contribute to decision making within the class and group		

Key Skills		Student rating	Briefly Explain
Being positive about learning			
I can ...	Find enjoyment and fun in learning		
	Learn from my mistakes and move on		
	Stick with things and work them through until I succeed		
	Recognise and celebrate my achievements		

Communicating

1 Poor   **2** Fair   **3** Good   **4** Very Good   **5** Excellent

Key Skills		Student rating	Briefly Explain
Listening and expressing myself			
I can ...	Listen actively		
	Express what I think and feel clearly in an appropriate tone		
	Agree and disagree respectfully		

1 Poor   **2** Fair   **3** Good   **4** Very Good   **5** Excellent

Key Skills		Student rating	Briefly Explain
	Ask well-thought-out questions and listen to the answer		
	Use different styles of communication		

Performing and presenting

I can ...	Express my ideas through presentation such as design and graphics		
	Make choices about how I can best present my ideas to others		

Discussing and debating

I can ...	Participate confidently in class discussion		
	Present my point of view and be able to explain and support it		
	Respond to opposite arguments constructively		

Using numbers and data

I can ...	Present, interpret and compare information using charts/diagrams		

Being Creative

1 Poor   **2** Fair   **3** Good   **4** Very Good   **5** Excellent

Key Skills		Student rating	Briefly Explain
Imagining			
I can ...	Use different ways of learning to help develop my imagination		
Exploring options and alternatives			
I can ...	Think through a problem step-by-step		
	Try different approaches when working on a task		
	Seek out different viewpoints and consider them carefully		
	Repeat the whole exercise if necessary		
Implementing ideas and taking action			
I can ...	See things through to completion		
	Evaluate different ideas		
Learning creatively			
I can ...	Participate in learning in creative ways		
	Suggest creative ways that help me to learn		

Working with Others

1 Poor   **2** Fair   **3** Good   **4** Very Good   **5** Excellent

Key Skills		Student rating	Briefly Explain
Developing good relationships and dealing with conflict			
I can ...	Share my ideas honestly		
	Show respect for different points of view		
	Give and receive praise and criticism constructively		
Co-operating			
I can ...	Show appreciation for the contribution of other group members		
	Contribute to decisions as part of a group		
Learning with others			
I can ...	Work in pairs and larger groups to help each other when we are learning		
	Help other students to understand and solve problems		
	Recognise that others can support my learning and know how to get their support		

313

Managing Information and Thinking

1 Poor   **2** Fair   **3** Good   **4** Very Good   **5** Excellent

Key Skills		Student rating	Briefly Explain
Being curious			
I can ...	Look for new and different ways of answering questions and solving problems		
	Ask questions to probe more deeply		
Gathering, recording, organising and evaluating information and data			
I can ...	Recognise what I already know		
	Analyse information and data presented in a variety of forms		
	Prepare and organise information and data so it makes sense to me and others		
Thinking creatively and critically			
I can ...	Question ideas and assumptions		
	Make connections between what I already know and new information		
	Adjust my thinking in light of new information		

① Poor **②** Fair **③** Good **④** Very Good **⑤** Excellent

Key Skills		Student rating	Briefly Explain
Reflecting on and evaluating my learning			
I can ...	Reflect on and review my own progress		
	Identify barriers to my learning and suggest ways of overcoming them		
	Use a range of tools to help manage my learning		
	Keep believing that with continued effort I can succeed.		
Using ICT and digital media to access, manage and share content			
I can ...	Use different technologies and digital media tools to give and receive feedback		

1.   Name three things you learned in this section?

     a. _____

     b. _____

     c. _____

2.   What three things did you enjoy the most in this section?

     a. _____

     b. _____

     c. _____

     Why did you enjoy these?

     _____

     _____

3.   Outline the three things which you found most difficult or
     challenging.

     a. _____

     b. _____

     c. _____

4.   Name three things you have taken from this section and have
     begun to use in your other subjects.

     a. _____

     b. _____

     c. _____

NOTES

Section 4
Study Journal

		Plan it		Do it		Review it				

Subject:				
Topic	**Level of difficulty**	**Notes Created on**	**POKER**	**1 Hour**	**1 Day**	**1 Week**	**1 Month**	**3 Months**	**Pre-Exam**
1	☆☆☆☆		☐	☐	☐	☐	☐	☐	☐
2	☆☆☆☆		☐	☐	☐	☐	☐	☐	☐
3	☆☆☆☆		☐	☐	☐	☐	☐	☐	☐
4	☆☆☆☆		☐	☐	☐	☐	☐	☐	☐
5	☆☆☆☆		☐	☐	☐	☐	☐	☐	☐
6	☆☆☆☆		☐	☐	☐	☐	☐	☐	☐
7	☆☆☆☆		☐	☐	☐	☐	☐	☐	☐
8	☆☆☆☆		☐	☐	☐	☐	☐	☐	☐
9	☆☆☆☆		☐	☐	☐	☐	☐	☐	☐
10	☆☆☆☆		☐	☐	☐	☐	☐	☐	☐
11	☆☆☆☆		☐	☐	☐	☐	☐	☐	☐
12	☆☆☆☆		☐	☐	☐	☐	☐	☐	☐
13	☆☆☆☆		☐	☐	☐	☐	☐	☐	☐
14	☆☆☆☆		☐	☐	☐	☐	☐	☐	☐
15	☆☆☆☆		☐	☐	☐	☐	☐	☐	☐
16	☆☆☆☆		☐	☐	☐	☐	☐	☐	☐
17	☆☆☆☆		☐	☐	☐	☐	☐	☐	☐
18	☆☆☆☆		☐	☐	☐	☐	☐	☐	☐
19	☆☆☆☆		☐	☐	☐	☐	☐	☐	☐
20	☆☆☆☆		☐	☐	☐	☐	☐	☐	☐

Section 4 - Study Journal

Plan it		Do it	Review it					

Subject:	Level of difficulty	Notes Created on	POKER	1 Hour	1 Day	1 Week	1 Month	3 Months	Pre-Exam
Topic									
1	☆☆☆☆		☐	☐	☐	☐	☐	☐	☐
2	☆☆☆☆		☐	☐	☐	☐	☐	☐	☐
3	☆☆☆☆		☐	☐	☐	☐	☐	☐	☐
4	☆☆☆☆		☐	☐	☐	☐	☐	☐	☐
5	☆☆☆☆		☐	☐	☐	☐	☐	☐	☐
6	☆☆☆☆		☐	☐	☐	☐	☐	☐	☐
7	☆☆☆☆		☐	☐	☐	☐	☐	☐	☐
8	☆☆☆☆		☐	☐	☐	☐	☐	☐	☐
9	☆☆☆☆		☐	☐	☐	☐	☐	☐	☐
10	☆☆☆☆		☐	☐	☐	☐	☐	☐	☐
11	☆☆☆☆		☐	☐	☐	☐	☐	☐	☐
12	☆☆☆☆		☐	☐	☐	☐	☐	☐	☐
13	☆☆☆☆		☐	☐	☐	☐	☐	☐	☐
14	☆☆☆☆		☐	☐	☐	☐	☐	☐	☐
15	☆☆☆☆		☐	☐	☐	☐	☐	☐	☐
16	☆☆☆☆		☐	☐	☐	☐	☐	☐	☐
17	☆☆☆☆		☐	☐	☐	☐	☐	☐	☐
18	☆☆☆☆		☐	☐	☐	☐	☐	☐	☐
19	☆☆☆☆		☐	☐	☐	☐	☐	☐	☐
20	☆☆☆☆		☐	☐	☐	☐	☐	☐	☐

			Plan it		Do it		Review it					

Subject:												
Topic	**Level of difficulty**	**Notes Created on**	**POKER**	**1 Hour**	**1 Day**	**1 Week**	**1 Month**	**3 Months**	**Pre-Exam**
1	☆☆☆☆		☐	☐	☐	☐	☐	☐	☐
2	☆☆☆☆		☐	☐	☐	☐	☐	☐	☐
3	☆☆☆☆		☐	☐	☐	☐	☐	☐	☐
4	☆☆☆☆		☐	☐	☐	☐	☐	☐	☐
5	☆☆☆☆		☐	☐	☐	☐	☐	☐	☐
6	☆☆☆☆		☐	☐	☐	☐	☐	☐	☐
7	☆☆☆☆		☐	☐	☐	☐	☐	☐	☐
8	☆☆☆☆		☐	☐	☐	☐	☐	☐	☐
9	☆☆☆☆		☐	☐	☐	☐	☐	☐	☐
10	☆☆☆☆		☐	☐	☐	☐	☐	☐	☐
11	☆☆☆☆		☐	☐	☐	☐	☐	☐	☐
12	☆☆☆☆		☐	☐	☐	☐	☐	☐	☐
13	☆☆☆☆		☐	☐	☐	☐	☐	☐	☐
14	☆☆☆☆		☐	☐	☐	☐	☐	☐	☐
15	☆☆☆☆		☐	☐	☐	☐	☐	☐	☐
16	☆☆☆☆		☐	☐	☐	☐	☐	☐	☐
17	☆☆☆☆		☐	☐	☐	☐	☐	☐	☐
18	☆☆☆☆		☐	☐	☐	☐	☐	☐	☐
19	☆☆☆☆		☐	☐	☐	☐	☐	☐	☐
20	☆☆☆☆		☐	☐	☐	☐	☐	☐	☐

Plan it		Do it	Review it					

		Level of difficulty	Notes Created on	POKER	1 Hour	1 Day	1 Week	1 Month	3 Months	Pre-Exam
Subject:	**Topic**									
1		☆☆☆☆		☐	☐	☐	☐	☐	☐	☐
2		☆☆☆☆		☐	☐	☐	☐	☐	☐	☐
3		☆☆☆☆		☐	☐	☐	☐	☐	☐	☐
4		☆☆☆☆		☐	☐	☐	☐	☐	☐	☐
5		☆☆☆☆		☐	☐	☐	☐	☐	☐	☐
6		☆☆☆☆		☐	☐	☐	☐	☐	☐	☐
7		☆☆☆☆		☐	☐	☐	☐	☐	☐	☐
8		☆☆☆☆		☐	☐	☐	☐	☐	☐	☐
9		☆☆☆☆		☐	☐	☐	☐	☐	☐	☐
10		☆☆☆☆		☐	☐	☐	☐	☐	☐	☐
11		☆☆☆☆		☐	☐	☐	☐	☐	☐	☐
12		☆☆☆☆		☐	☐	☐	☐	☐	☐	☐
13		☆☆☆☆		☐	☐	☐	☐	☐	☐	☐
14		☆☆☆☆		☐	☐	☐	☐	☐	☐	☐
15		☆☆☆☆		☐	☐	☐	☐	☐	☐	☐
16		☆☆☆☆		☐	☐	☐	☐	☐	☐	☐
17		☆☆☆☆		☐	☐	☐	☐	☐	☐	☐
18		☆☆☆☆		☐	☐	☐	☐	☐	☐	☐
19		☆☆☆☆		☐	☐	☐	☐	☐	☐	☐
20		☆☆☆☆		☐	☐	☐	☐	☐	☐	☐

	Plan it			Do it	Review it					

Subject:	Level of difficulty	Notes Created on	POKER	1 Hour	1 Day	1 Week	1 Month	3 Months	Pre-Exam
Topic									
1	☆☆☆☆		☐	☐	☐	☐	☐	☐	☐
2	☆☆☆☆		☐	☐	☐	☐	☐	☐	☐
3	☆☆☆☆		☐	☐	☐	☐	☐	☐	☐
4	☆☆☆☆		☐	☐	☐	☐	☐	☐	☐
5	☆☆☆☆		☐	☐	☐	☐	☐	☐	☐
6	☆☆☆☆		☐	☐	☐	☐	☐	☐	☐
7	☆☆☆☆		☐	☐	☐	☐	☐	☐	☐
8	☆☆☆☆		☐	☐	☐	☐	☐	☐	☐
9	☆☆☆☆		☐	☐	☐	☐	☐	☐	☐
10	☆☆☆☆		☐	☐	☐	☐	☐	☐	☐
11	☆☆☆☆		☐	☐	☐	☐	☐	☐	☐
12	☆☆☆☆		☐	☐	☐	☐	☐	☐	☐
13	☆☆☆☆		☐	☐	☐	☐	☐	☐	☐
14	☆☆☆☆		☐	☐	☐	☐	☐	☐	☐
15	☆☆☆☆		☐	☐	☐	☐	☐	☐	☐
16	☆☆☆☆		☐	☐	☐	☐	☐	☐	☐
17	☆☆☆☆		☐	☐	☐	☐	☐	☐	☐
18	☆☆☆☆		☐	☐	☐	☐	☐	☐	☐
19	☆☆☆☆		☐	☐	☐	☐	☐	☐	☐
20	☆☆☆☆		☐	☐	☐	☐	☐	☐	☐

Section 4 - Study Journal

	Plan it		Do it	Review it					
Subject:	Level of difficulty	Notes Created on	POKER	1 Hour	1 Day	1 Week	1 Month	3 Months	Pre-Exam
Topic									
1	☆☆☆☆		☐	☐	☐	☐	☐	☐	☐
2	☆☆☆☆		☐	☐	☐	☐	☐	☐	☐
3	☆☆☆☆		☐	☐	☐	☐	☐	☐	☐
4	☆☆☆☆		☐	☐	☐	☐	☐	☐	☐
5	☆☆☆☆		☐	☐	☐	☐	☐	☐	☐
6	☆☆☆☆		☐	☐	☐	☐	☐	☐	☐
7	☆☆☆☆		☐	☐	☐	☐	☐	☐	☐
8	☆☆☆☆		☐	☐	☐	☐	☐	☐	☐
9	☆☆☆☆		☐	☐	☐	☐	☐	☐	☐
10	☆☆☆☆		☐	☐	☐	☐	☐	☐	☐
11	☆☆☆☆		☐	☐	☐	☐	☐	☐	☐
12	☆☆☆☆		☐	☐	☐	☐	☐	☐	☐
13	☆☆☆☆		☐	☐	☐	☐	☐	☐	☐
14	☆☆☆☆		☐	☐	☐	☐	☐	☐	☐
15	☆☆☆☆		☐	☐	☐	☐	☐	☐	☐
16	☆☆☆☆		☐	☐	☐	☐	☐	☐	☐
17	☆☆☆☆		☐	☐	☐	☐	☐	☐	☐
18	☆☆☆☆		☐	☐	☐	☐	☐	☐	☐
19	☆☆☆☆		☐	☐	☐	☐	☐	☐	☐
20	☆☆☆☆		☐	☐	☐	☐	☐	☐	☐

	Plan it		Do it	Review it					

Subject:									
Topic	Level of difficulty	Notes Created on	POKER	1 Hour	1 Day	1 Week	1 Month	3 Months	Pre-Exam
1	☆☆☆☆		☐	☐	☐	☐	☐	☐	☐
2	☆☆☆☆		☐	☐	☐	☐	☐	☐	☐
3	☆☆☆☆		☐	☐	☐	☐	☐	☐	☐
4	☆☆☆☆		☐	☐	☐	☐	☐	☐	☐
5	☆☆☆☆		☐	☐	☐	☐	☐	☐	☐
6	☆☆☆☆		☐	☐	☐	☐	☐	☐	☐
7	☆☆☆☆		☐	☐	☐	☐	☐	☐	☐
8	☆☆☆☆		☐	☐	☐	☐	☐	☐	☐
9	☆☆☆☆		☐	☐	☐	☐	☐	☐	☐
10	☆☆☆☆		☐	☐	☐	☐	☐	☐	☐
11	☆☆☆☆		☐	☐	☐	☐	☐	☐	☐
12	☆☆☆☆		☐	☐	☐	☐	☐	☐	☐
13	☆☆☆☆		☐	☐	☐	☐	☐	☐	☐
14	☆☆☆☆		☐	☐	☐	☐	☐	☐	☐
15	☆☆☆☆		☐	☐	☐	☐	☐	☐	☐
16	☆☆☆☆		☐	☐	☐	☐	☐	☐	☐
17	☆☆☆☆		☐	☐	☐	☐	☐	☐	☐
18	☆☆☆☆		☐	☐	☐	☐	☐	☐	☐
19	☆☆☆☆		☐	☐	☐	☐	☐	☐	☐
20	☆☆☆☆		☐	☐	☐	☐	☐	☐	☐

Section 4 - Study Journal

| Plan it | | Do it | Review it | | | | | |

Subject:	Level of difficulty	Notes Created on	POKER	1 Hour	1 Day	1 Week	1 Month	3 Months	Pre-Exam
Topic									
1	☆☆☆☆		☐	☐	☐	☐	☐	☐	☐
2	☆☆☆☆		☐	☐	☐	☐	☐	☐	☐
3	☆☆☆☆		☐	☐	☐	☐	☐	☐	☐
4	☆☆☆☆		☐	☐	☐	☐	☐	☐	☐
5	☆☆☆☆		☐	☐	☐	☐	☐	☐	☐
6	☆☆☆☆		☐	☐	☐	☐	☐	☐	☐
7	☆☆☆☆		☐	☐	☐	☐	☐	☐	☐
8	☆☆☆☆		☐	☐	☐	☐	☐	☐	☐
9	☆☆☆☆		☐	☐	☐	☐	☐	☐	☐
10	☆☆☆☆		☐	☐	☐	☐	☐	☐	☐
11	☆☆☆☆		☐	☐	☐	☐	☐	☐	☐
12	☆☆☆☆		☐	☐	☐	☐	☐	☐	☐
13	☆☆☆☆		☐	☐	☐	☐	☐	☐	☐
14	☆☆☆☆		☐	☐	☐	☐	☐	☐	☐
15	☆☆☆☆		☐	☐	☐	☐	☐	☐	☐
16	☆☆☆☆		☐	☐	☐	☐	☐	☐	☐
17	☆☆☆☆		☐	☐	☐	☐	☐	☐	☐
18	☆☆☆☆		☐	☐	☐	☐	☐	☐	☐
19	☆☆☆☆		☐	☐	☐	☐	☐	☐	☐
20	☆☆☆☆		☐	☐	☐	☐	☐	☐	☐

	Plan it			Do it	Review it					
Subject:		**Level of difficulty**	**Notes Created on**	**POKER**	**1 Hour**	**1 Day**	**1 Week**	**1 Month**	**3 Months**	**Pre-Exam**
Topic										
1		☆☆☆☆		☐	☐	☐	☐	☐	☐	☐
2		☆☆☆☆		☐	☐	☐	☐	☐	☐	☐
3		☆☆☆☆		☐	☐	☐	☐	☐	☐	☐
4		☆☆☆☆		☐	☐	☐	☐	☐	☐	☐
5		☆☆☆☆		☐	☐	☐	☐	☐	☐	☐
6		☆☆☆☆		☐	☐	☐	☐	☐	☐	☐
7		☆☆☆☆		☐	☐	☐	☐	☐	☐	☐
8		☆☆☆☆		☐	☐	☐	☐	☐	☐	☐
9		☆☆☆☆		☐	☐	☐	☐	☐	☐	☐
10		☆☆☆☆		☐	☐	☐	☐	☐	☐	☐
11		☆☆☆☆		☐	☐	☐	☐	☐	☐	☐
12		☆☆☆☆		☐	☐	☐	☐	☐	☐	☐
13		☆☆☆☆		☐	☐	☐	☐	☐	☐	☐
14		☆☆☆☆		☐	☐	☐	☐	☐	☐	☐
15		☆☆☆☆		☐	☐	☐	☐	☐	☐	☐
16		☆☆☆☆		☐	☐	☐	☐	☐	☐	☐
17		☆☆☆☆		☐	☐	☐	☐	☐	☐	☐
18		☆☆☆☆		☐	☐	☐	☐	☐	☐	☐
19		☆☆☆☆		☐	☐	☐	☐	☐	☐	☐
20		☆☆☆☆		☐	☐	☐	☐	☐	☐	☐

Section 4 - Study Journal

| Plan it | | | Do it | Review it | | | | | |

Subject:	Level of difficulty	Notes Created on	POKER	1 Hour	1 Day	1 Week	1 Month	3 Months	Pre-Exam
Topic									
1	☆☆☆☆		☐	☐	☐	☐	☐	☐	☐
2	☆☆☆☆		☐	☐	☐	☐	☐	☐	☐
3	☆☆☆☆		☐	☐	☐	☐	☐	☐	☐
4	☆☆☆☆		☐	☐	☐	☐	☐	☐	☐
5	☆☆☆☆		☐	☐	☐	☐	☐	☐	☐
6	☆☆☆☆		☐	☐	☐	☐	☐	☐	☐
7	☆☆☆☆		☐	☐	☐	☐	☐	☐	☐
8	☆☆☆☆		☐	☐	☐	☐	☐	☐	☐
9	☆☆☆☆		☐	☐	☐	☐	☐	☐	☐
10	☆☆☆☆		☐	☐	☐	☐	☐	☐	☐
11	☆☆☆☆		☐	☐	☐	☐	☐	☐	☐
12	☆☆☆☆		☐	☐	☐	☐	☐	☐	☐
13	☆☆☆☆		☐	☐	☐	☐	☐	☐	☐
14	☆☆☆☆		☐	☐	☐	☐	☐	☐	☐
15	☆☆☆☆		☐	☐	☐	☐	☐	☐	☐
16	☆☆☆☆		☐	☐	☐	☐	☐	☐	☐
17	☆☆☆☆		☐	☐	☐	☐	☐	☐	☐
18	☆☆☆☆		☐	☐	☐	☐	☐	☐	☐
19	☆☆☆☆		☐	☐	☐	☐	☐	☐	☐
20	☆☆☆☆		☐	☐	☐	☐	☐	☐	☐

	Plan it			Do it		Review it					
Subject:											
Topic		Level of difficulty	Notes Created on	POKER	1 Hour	1 Day	1 Week	1 Month	3 Months	Pre-Exam
1		☆☆☆☆		☐	☐	☐	☐	☐	☐	☐
2		☆☆☆☆		☐	☐	☐	☐	☐	☐	☐
3		☆☆☆☆		☐	☐	☐	☐	☐	☐	☐
4		☆☆☆☆		☐	☐	☐	☐	☐	☐	☐
5		☆☆☆☆		☐	☐	☐	☐	☐	☐	☐
6		☆☆☆☆		☐	☐	☐	☐	☐	☐	☐
7		☆☆☆☆		☐	☐	☐	☐	☐	☐	☐
8		☆☆☆☆		☐	☐	☐	☐	☐	☐	☐
9		☆☆☆☆		☐	☐	☐	☐	☐	☐	☐
10		☆☆☆☆		☐	☐	☐	☐	☐	☐	☐
11		☆☆☆☆		☐	☐	☐	☐	☐	☐	☐
12		☆☆☆☆		☐	☐	☐	☐	☐	☐	☐
13		☆☆☆☆		☐	☐	☐	☐	☐	☐	☐
14		☆☆☆☆		☐	☐	☐	☐	☐	☐	☐
15		☆☆☆☆		☐	☐	☐	☐	☐	☐	☐
16		☆☆☆☆		☐	☐	☐	☐	☐	☐	☐
17		☆☆☆☆		☐	☐	☐	☐	☐	☐	☐
18		☆☆☆☆		☐	☐	☐	☐	☐	☐	☐
19		☆☆☆☆		☐	☐	☐	☐	☐	☐	☐
20		☆☆☆☆		☐	☐	☐	☐	☐	☐	☐

Section 4 - Study Journal

| Plan it | | Do it | Review it | | | | | | |

Subject:	Level of difficulty	Notes Created on	POKER	1 Hour	1 Day	1 Week	1 Month	3 Months	Pre-Exam
Topic									
1	☆☆☆☆		☐	☐	☐	☐	☐	☐	☐
2	☆☆☆☆		☐	☐	☐	☐	☐	☐	☐
3	☆☆☆☆		☐	☐	☐	☐	☐	☐	☐
4	☆☆☆☆		☐	☐	☐	☐	☐	☐	☐
5	☆☆☆☆		☐	☐	☐	☐	☐	☐	☐
6	☆☆☆☆		☐	☐	☐	☐	☐	☐	☐
7	☆☆☆☆		☐	☐	☐	☐	☐	☐	☐
8	☆☆☆☆		☐	☐	☐	☐	☐	☐	☐
9	☆☆☆☆		☐	☐	☐	☐	☐	☐	☐
10	☆☆☆☆		☐	☐	☐	☐	☐	☐	☐
11	☆☆☆☆		☐	☐	☐	☐	☐	☐	☐
12	☆☆☆☆		☐	☐	☐	☐	☐	☐	☐
13	☆☆☆☆		☐	☐	☐	☐	☐	☐	☐
14	☆☆☆☆		☐	☐	☐	☐	☐	☐	☐
15	☆☆☆☆		☐	☐	☐	☐	☐	☐	☐
16	☆☆☆☆		☐	☐	☐	☐	☐	☐	☐
17	☆☆☆☆		☐	☐	☐	☐	☐	☐	☐
18	☆☆☆☆		☐	☐	☐	☐	☐	☐	☐
19	☆☆☆☆		☐	☐	☐	☐	☐	☐	☐
20	☆☆☆☆		☐	☐	☐	☐	☐	☐	☐

	Plan it			Do it		Review it					

Subject:											
Topic	Level of difficulty	Notes Created on	POKER	1 Hour	1 Day	1 Week	1 Month	3 Months	Pre-Exam
1	☆☆☆☆		☐	☐	☐	☐	☐	☐	☐
2	☆☆☆☆		☐	☐	☐	☐	☐	☐	☐
3	☆☆☆☆		☐	☐	☐	☐	☐	☐	☐
4	☆☆☆☆		☐	☐	☐	☐	☐	☐	☐
5	☆☆☆☆		☐	☐	☐	☐	☐	☐	☐
6	☆☆☆☆		☐	☐	☐	☐	☐	☐	☐
7	☆☆☆☆		☐	☐	☐	☐	☐	☐	☐
8	☆☆☆☆		☐	☐	☐	☐	☐	☐	☐
9	☆☆☆☆		☐	☐	☐	☐	☐	☐	☐
10	☆☆☆☆		☐	☐	☐	☐	☐	☐	☐
11	☆☆☆☆		☐	☐	☐	☐	☐	☐	☐
12	☆☆☆☆		☐	☐	☐	☐	☐	☐	☐
13	☆☆☆☆		☐	☐	☐	☐	☐	☐	☐
14	☆☆☆☆		☐	☐	☐	☐	☐	☐	☐
15	☆☆☆☆		☐	☐	☐	☐	☐	☐	☐
16	☆☆☆☆		☐	☐	☐	☐	☐	☐	☐
17	☆☆☆☆		☐	☐	☐	☐	☐	☐	☐
18	☆☆☆☆		☐	☐	☐	☐	☐	☐	☐
19	☆☆☆☆		☐	☐	☐	☐	☐	☐	☐
20	☆☆☆☆		☐	☐	☐	☐	☐	☐	☐

Section 4 - Study Journal

Plan it		Do it	Review it						

Subject:										
Topic	Level of difficulty	Notes Created on	POKER	1 Hour	1 Day	1 Week	1 Month	3 Months	Pre-Exam
1	☆☆☆☆		☐	☐	☐	☐	☐	☐	☐
2	☆☆☆☆		☐	☐	☐	☐	☐	☐	☐
3	☆☆☆☆		☐	☐	☐	☐	☐	☐	☐
4	☆☆☆☆		☐	☐	☐	☐	☐	☐	☐
5	☆☆☆☆		☐	☐	☐	☐	☐	☐	☐
6	☆☆☆☆		☐	☐	☐	☐	☐	☐	☐
7	☆☆☆☆		☐	☐	☐	☐	☐	☐	☐
8	☆☆☆☆		☐	☐	☐	☐	☐	☐	☐
9	☆☆☆☆		☐	☐	☐	☐	☐	☐	☐
10	☆☆☆☆		☐	☐	☐	☐	☐	☐	☐
11	☆☆☆☆		☐	☐	☐	☐	☐	☐	☐
12	☆☆☆☆		☐	☐	☐	☐	☐	☐	☐
13	☆☆☆☆		☐	☐	☐	☐	☐	☐	☐
14	☆☆☆☆		☐	☐	☐	☐	☐	☐	☐
15	☆☆☆☆		☐	☐	☐	☐	☐	☐	☐
16	☆☆☆☆		☐	☐	☐	☐	☐	☐	☐
17	☆☆☆☆		☐	☐	☐	☐	☐	☐	☐
18	☆☆☆☆		☐	☐	☐	☐	☐	☐	☐
19	☆☆☆☆		☐	☐	☐	☐	☐	☐	☐
20	☆☆☆☆		☐	☐	☐	☐	☐	☐	☐

	Plan it		Do it	Review it					

Subject:	Level of difficulty	Notes Created on	POKER	1 Hour	1 Day	1 Week	1 Month	3 Months	Pre-Exam
Topic									
1	☆☆☆☆		☐	☐	☐	☐	☐	☐	☐
2	☆☆☆☆		☐	☐	☐	☐	☐	☐	☐
3	☆☆☆☆		☐	☐	☐	☐	☐	☐	☐
4	☆☆☆☆		☐	☐	☐	☐	☐	☐	☐
5	☆☆☆☆		☐	☐	☐	☐	☐	☐	☐
6	☆☆☆☆		☐	☐	☐	☐	☐	☐	☐
7	☆☆☆☆		☐	☐	☐	☐	☐	☐	☐
8	☆☆☆☆		☐	☐	☐	☐	☐	☐	☐
9	☆☆☆☆		☐	☐	☐	☐	☐	☐	☐
10	☆☆☆☆		☐	☐	☐	☐	☐	☐	☐
11	☆☆☆☆		☐	☐	☐	☐	☐	☐	☐
12	☆☆☆☆		☐	☐	☐	☐	☐	☐	☐
13	☆☆☆☆		☐	☐	☐	☐	☐	☐	☐
14	☆☆☆☆		☐	☐	☐	☐	☐	☐	☐
15	☆☆☆☆		☐	☐	☐	☐	☐	☐	☐
16	☆☆☆☆		☐	☐	☐	☐	☐	☐	☐
17	☆☆☆☆		☐	☐	☐	☐	☐	☐	☐
18	☆☆☆☆		☐	☐	☐	☐	☐	☐	☐
19	☆☆☆☆		☐	☐	☐	☐	☐	☐	☐
20	☆☆☆☆		☐	☐	☐	☐	☐	☐	☐

Section 4 - Weekly Timetable

SUN

Time

SAT

Time

FRI

Time

THU

Time

WED

Time

TUE

Time

MON

Time

SUN

Time

SAT

Time

FRI

Time

THU

Time

WED

Time

TUE

Time

MON

Time

Section 4 - Year Planner

	September		October		November		December		January	
	Time Homework	Time Study	Time Homework	Time Study	Time Homework	Time Study	Time Homework	Time Study	Time Homework	Time Study
1										
2										
3										
4										
5										
6										
7										
8										
9										
10										
11										
12										
13										
14										
15										
16										
17										
18										
19										
20										
21										
22										
23										
24										
25										
26										
27										
28										
29										
30										
31										
Total time			Total time		Total time		Total time		Total time	